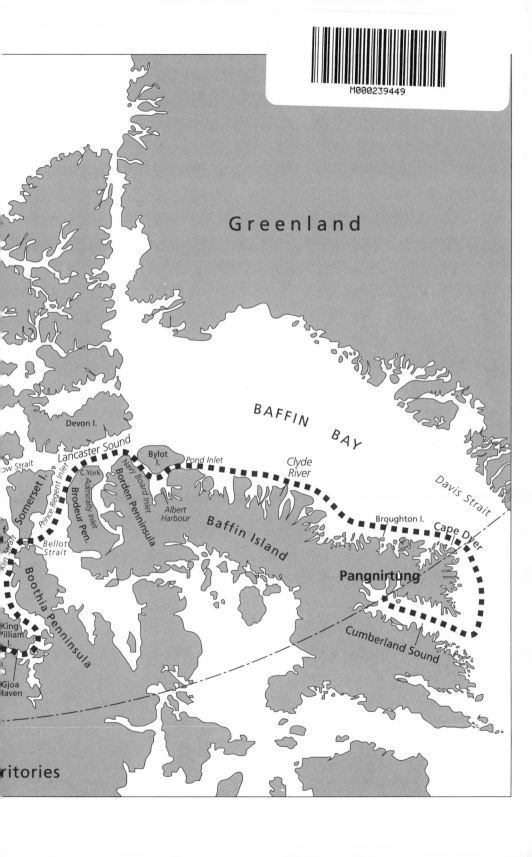

PUBLISHER'S NOTE

Publishers rarely get manuscripts of historical importance "over the transom," especially ones done in calligraphy, with beautiful illustrations, about striking deeds of unusual adventure and courage. *Arctic Odyssey* is such a book.

In a time when corporate sponsorship and media hype dull our senses, we find it satisfying to know that three Canadian friends can each put $400 into a food kitty and sail off in a 27-foot homemade boat to do what most arctic explorers would consider unthinkable. Strong-willed Captain Winston Bushnell designed and built his steel sloop, *Dove III,* then set forth, not on a whim, but on a carefully-planned voyage through the famed Northwest Passage. This world circumnavigator brought his boat and crew through the icy waters, making them the fourth yacht in history to transit the Passage in a single season. Only 57 vessels, including atomic icebreakers, have ever completed the Northwest Passage.

With this superior feat of seamanship and daring, *Dove*'s captain and crew— Bushnell, George Hone, and Len Sherman—have joined a select group of arctic yachtsmen led by Willy de Roos, who sailed in 1977 from a point on the Arctic Circle off Greenland to the Arctic Circle off Alaska, a distance of 4,000 nautical miles—the first single-season transit.

By chance, *Dove III* met up with *The Croatian Tern,* captained by Mladen Sutej, near the halfway point in the Northwest Passage. Sutej's expedition was fully sponsored, with all the high-tech gear imaginable, but ironically his passage ended less than one week later than *Dove*, making *The Croatian Tern* the fifth boat to complete the Northwest Passage in a single season.

ARCTIC ODYSSEY

Dove III Masters

the Northwest

Passage

Len Sherman

FineEdge.com

Copyright © 1999 by Len Sherman

Book design by Faith Rumm and Melanie Haage
Inside maps by the author
Illustrations by the author
Copyediting by Cindy Kamler

Library of Congress Cataloging in Publication Data

Sherman, Len, 1941–
    Arctic odyssey : Dove III masters the Northwest Passage / by Len
Sherman.
        p.   cm.
    ISBN 0-938665-63-4
    1. Sherman, Len, 1941–   --Journeys--Arctic regions.   2. Dove III
(Sailing vessel)   3. Northwest Passage.   4. Arctic regions--Description
and travel.   I. Title.
G650 1995.S48   1999   99-19622
910'.9163'27--DC21   CIP

ISBN 0-938665-63-4

Published by Fine Edge Productions/FineEdge.com

Address requests for permission to:
Fine Edge Productions/FineEdge.com
mail@FineEdge.com

Printed in Canada
First Edition

To San
for an abundance of patience,
understanding and inspiration.
You're an artist's dream come true.

Preparations for the Journey

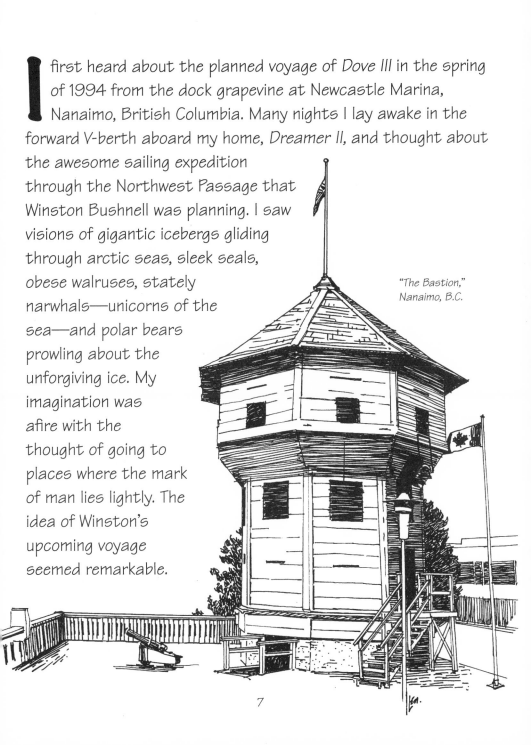

I first heard about the planned voyage of *Dove III* in the spring of 1994 from the dock grapevine at Newcastle Marina, Nanaimo, British Columbia. Many nights I lay awake in the forward V-berth aboard my home, *Dreamer II*, and thought about the awesome sailing expedition through the Northwest Passage that Winston Bushnell was planning. I saw visions of gigantic icebergs gliding through arctic seas, sleek seals, obese walruses, stately narwhals—unicorns of the sea—and polar bears prowling about the unforgiving ice. My imagination was afire with the thought of going to places where the mark of man lies lightly. The idea of Winston's upcoming voyage seemed remarkable.

"The Bastion," Nanaimo, B.C.

The more I thought about this voyage, the more intrigued I was until at last I mustered up the courage to ask if Winston needed any additional crew. I was understandably apprehensive because at best I was a novice sailor, barely a step above "land-lubber." Winston's original plan included only one other person, one he had already found in the very capable and experienced 36-year-old George Hone.

However, much to my surprise and delight, I was accepted—mainly because a previous crew of two said that their recent successful traversal of the Northwest Passage would have been easier with three people; at times both of them had to stay awake for 40 hours at a stretch in order to safely maneuver their boat through the labyrinth of openings in the ice. "And besides," Winston proclaimed with a sly grin, "I don't have to worry about you mutinying."

I felt honored to be one of his crew, but I admit that there were many times before and during the voyage when I shook my head and asked myself: "What in the world are you doing, Len?"

The first time I met Winston Bushnell was at my 50th birthday party, where he promptly pushed my face into my cake. I recall being irked at first, but how can you fail to like a person whose wide, contagious smile would stretch to the back of his head if it wasn't for his ears. There is also a pronounced, mischievous glee in his twinkling blue eyes; at age 58, he is a man to be revered for his courage and seamanship over the past 30 years.

Imagine, if you can, limping into Cape Town, South Africa, under jury-rig (temporary mast) aboard a tiny 10-meter sail-boat which had been dismasted after twice being rolled over, then knocked down two more times by gargantuan waves off the west coast of Africa. That near-disaster had left his wife, Carolynne, and two teen-age daughters, Leslie and Kim, bailing for their lives below decks while Winston battled the elements topside. With only $15 in their pockets and a badly damaged boat to repair, most people would have said, "I'm outta here!" But not the Bushnells. After rebuilding and refitting

Dove's captain, Winston Bushnell

Dove over a 14-month period, they were off again. In addition to the two girls, they now had a three-month-old son, Stevie.

I had been accepted as part of the crew, but I still had to give myself the occasional pinch to make sure this was really happening. Then the unspeakable occurred—doubt arose. Yes, that destructive, negative feeling began to nibble at me, erod-ing my uplifted spirits. Insecurities about my sailing experi-ence—or should I say lack of sailing experience—began to get the better of me. After all, Winston had sailed around the world while raising a family and had survived some of the worst sailing conditions imaginable. George, too, was an experienced seaman, having skippered and crewed on several lengthy offshore cruises.

Another worry I had to contend with was seasickness. I had heard of people who suffered continually during lengthy voyages and were diagnosed as chronically seasick. Never having sailed on the open ocean before, where the rollers are constantly moving up and down, up and down, I was concerned about how I would fare. On more than one occasion, I have experienced this malady while sailing on a lumpy sea. After all, I couldn't just step off the boat and go home if I didn't feel well. However, several well-seasoned sailors told me that they often came down with a bout of seasickness when a voyage began, but that after a few days they would feel their old selves again. I hoped it would be the same for me; the last thing I wanted was to be a burden.

Winston's Arctic expedition planned to navigate the legendary Northwest Passage from west to east. (The Northwest Passage is described as from the Arctic Circle (Bering Strait/Chukchi Sea) on the west to the Arctic Circle (Davis Strait) on the east.) Most successful voyages through the Passage have been made going east to west. Because there is only a very small window in the summer when the ice opens up, most of those who have succeeded sailed down along the west coast of King William Island through Queen Maud and Coronation gulfs to Amundsen Gulf and on to the Bering Strait. Since there are fewer islands scattered along this route, generally the going is easier, depending on the year's ice conditions. However, once a vessel is committed to sailing through the Passage, she's stuck if winter comes early! Most likely the vessel would have to remain until the ice opened up the following year, unless it had the aid of an ice-breaker.

What inspires a person to go sailing through the ice-laden

Northwest Passage? Men like Sir John Franklin and Roald Amundsen, who searched for a shorter avenue to the Orient in order to improve world trade and make scientific observations, mainly were doing their jobs. Even our own Sergeant Henry Larsen, Captain of the dauntless R.C.M.P. schooner, St. Roch , had a mission to accomplish during the Second World War. Other adventurers went, I'm sure, strictly for the prestige and glory. For me, it was neither a job, mission or glory, it was simply the trip of a lifetime—and I couldn't say no to that!

Some people, like Winston, have the sea in their blood. I've never really had a strong urge to go to sea, except maybe once. Around the young, impressionable age of 21, a friend and I almost signed aboard a Europe-bound freighter out of Vancouver, B.C. At the time it seemed a most romantic and adventurous endeavor. However, my steaming off to Europe was abruptly curtailed by the comments of another friend who had worked aboard an old freighter during World War II.

I can still see his long, gaunt face and sparse, disheveled red hair as he sat looking at me across a barroom table with a wildness in his eyes. Perhaps the beers he had drunk gave him this outlandish appearance, but I think not. On hearing his perilous wartime tales of crossing the North Atlantic to England, I was convinced that a similar experience could drive any man to drink. Although the convoys in which he travelled were protected by lethal warships, many of the freighters were attacked and sunk by the ever-present and deadly German U-boats. Whenever an enemy submarine was sighted, an alarm would ring through the ship. For my friend stoking coal in the red-hot boilers far below in the belly of the freighter, this was dire news. All the hatches leading to the engine rooms were instantly sealed, leaving no possible escape for the boiler crew. As he put it, "All me and my mates could do was shovel coal, wait and pray! A direct hit would have been merciful, otherwise we were fried, boiled or drowned. There was no way out!"

I don't know how many times I asked myself why I wanted to crew on such a long and arduous arctic voyage. Some of my friends thought I was mad. They said, "If it was me, I'd be sailing where it's a lot warmer." To be honest, I agreed with them, especially after reading accounts of several early arctic expeditions in search of the Northwest Passage, some of which concluded with tragic results. Three weeks before we sailed, I was still questioning my sanity.

Easter Monday, April 17, 1995

As I lie in bed with my wife Sandra snuggled warmly against my back, a kaleidoscope of thoughts turns inside my head. I can't help but think how foolish I must be to leave all the people I love most in this world to go on a journey, a dangerous journey from which I might never return. Life is so short and precious, why risk mine on a voyage for which I have no intelligent reasons or goals? Am I going through male menopause, some mid-life crisis, perhaps a search for my youth? I don't think so; I can't remember ever being so content. Perhaps that's it. There's no stress in my life so I've decided to throw in a dash of danger to spice it up.

April 22, 1995

Winston and I were enjoying a cup of tea at the Granary Cafe when the waitress asked why we were going on such a trip. Laughing, I blurted out,

"Because we're real men! We thrive on hardship and pain! We live for excitement and the chance to face death!" I was slightly taken aback when Winston replied quietly, "You know, for me, that's almost what it's all about."

The reasons why? The reasons why? Perhaps my main reason for wanting to traverse the Northwest Passage is as simple as the motto that Winston lives by, one with which I heartily agree: "Grab a chance and you won't be sorry for a might-have-been!"

For quite some time, Sandra, and I discussed the pros and cons of my going on such a lengthy and possibly dangerous voyage. Understandably, she was concerned for my safety, more so than for the amount of money such an endeavor would cost. Over the years, we had talked about going on an extended offshore cruise to a warmer climate such as Hawaii, Mexico or the South Pacific islands. Unfortunately, Sandra doesn't feel she is physically capable of such a voyage. Then again, maybe she's not too enthused about my sailing ability. I can't say I blame her on that count as the same doubts also crossed my mind.

As a some-of-the-time employed artist, I had earned a fair amount of money painting some murals for a German restaurant, but not enough for the entire journey. Realizing how much it meant to me, Sandra generously helped out with the trip's financing. Sandra had a full-time job working as a recreation therapist for people afflicted with dementia or physical disabilities. We knew her finances would be tight without my added income, but Sandra figured she would be all right until my return in the fall. Little did we know just how tight the situation would become. Had I known then, I probably wouldn't have gone.

Sandra is a real "smother-mother," and she was convinced the voyage would be terribly cold, so she spent hours sewing clothes for me from a material known as arctic fleece (seems appropriate). Besides the two pairs of pants and a jacket, she also sewed matching headbands decorated with doves for the three of us. Although the weather was warm for the most part, the clothes Sandra made kept me warm and comfy on some of the colder days near the end of the journey.

We both realized how much we would miss one another, especially when bedtime came. There's something about cuddling up to someone every night; it's just not the same when you sleep alone. I wasn't too worried about my daughters as they are grown, with lives of their own. My seven-year-old son lives in Victoria, B.C. with his mother and would scarcely notice I was gone, since I don't often get to see him.

What about *Dove III*, the little boat that was to be our home and "refuge from the storm" for almost 5 months? Like Winston's earlier boats, he built her himself on a very stringent budget. Come to think of it, Winston is like a mother; it took him nine months to build, christen, launch, and burp her—oops, I mean berth her. *Dove* (as we affectionately called her) is a

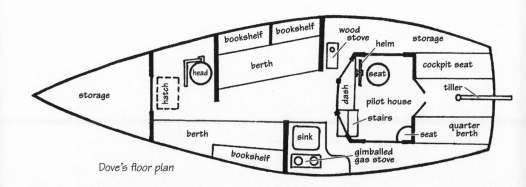

Dove's floor plan

10-gauge rugged steel, hard chine, shoal draft, sloop-rigged vessel, 8.5 meters long by 2.5 meters wide (beam), wherein beats a stout 23-hp Isuzu diesel for a heart. She boasts a comfortable pilothouse topside and an overwide keel at the base which houses a centerboard that draws 1.8 meters when lowered. I probably shouldn't mention this, as most people don't like their weight revealed; sorry, *Dove*, but you weigh in at a slim six tons.

Winston's original plan for sailing the Northwest Passage was for a two-year voyage divided into two separate legs. The first leg consisted of towing *Dove* on a trailer to Inuvik, Northwest Territories, and launching her in the Mackenzie River. After cruising down the river, we would sail her through the eastern section of the Northwest Passage to Davis Strait and then down the Labrador coast to Lake Erie. We would haul her out at Belleville, Ontario, and tow her to my brother's farm at Sterling, Alberta, for the following winter.

The following spring, *Dove* would again be towed to Inuvik. After sailing to the mouth of the Mackenzie River, we would sail her through the western portion of the Northwest Passage to the Bering Sea, then across the North Pacific to Vancouver Island and home.

However, the cost, as well as the dangers of hauling *Dove* via truck and trailer across thousands of kilometers of rough terrain, caused us to abandon that plan. Sailing the Northwest Passage from Nanaimo to Belleville in one season seemed more practical and economical.

As well as finalizing our route and schedule, a great many other preparations still had to be completed, including finishing the boat. When I first arrived on the scene, *Dove* was nothing but a hollow shell. I remember walking the deck and thinking: She sure doesn't look like much; boy, is she small.

While getting the nickel tour below decks, Winston introduced me to my future sleeping accommodation. My bunk or pipe berth, located near the port stern of the vessel on the pilot-house floor, looked like a half-open coffin. When Winston edged himself in, the only part of him I could see was his head lying underneath the small corner seat. The berth was adequate, but for someone like me, who sometimes awakens in a cold, clammy sweat from dreams of being trapped in total darkness and unable to move, this bed looked more like a living nightmare than a comfortable place to sleep.

During the voyage, the berth's tight restrictions made it impossible for me to turn over, so unless we were rotating bunks, I usually slept stretched out in the center of the pilot-house floor. However, at times when I couldn't use either George's or Winston's bunk because of our tack and sea conditions, this tight little berth became my haven.

While Winston worked on the boat, I began designing a brochure and pamphlet illustrating our prospective voyage in the hope of attaining much-needed sponsorship. I'm not comfortable asking people for something free, so I was apprehensive about approaching possible sponsors. Who to approach was another question. Sandra got the ball rolling by directing me to the Institute of Ocean Sciences where she once worked. All Canadian navigational charts are prepared at this Sidney, B.C. facility. Upon our arrival at the Institute, we were greeted cordially by several people who, at one time or another, had worked in the arctic regions of Canada. Not only did they have a keen interest in our future voyage, they also supplied us with vital information from their own arctic experiences.

When Sandra and I returned to Nanaimo, I hurried to tell Winston about our warm reception and the good possibility of sponsorship. Winston, George and I were soon knocking on the door of Mr. Tony O'Connor, Director of Hydrography for the Pacific Region. Being a man who had spent a considerable amount of time working in the Arctic, Tony was understandably intrigued by our upcoming voyage and approved the donation of any Canadian navigational charts that Winston deemed necessary for the success of the journey. These charts proved their worth when we were navigating the treacherously shallow and ice-encumbered waters of the Arctic.

Another lead was suggested by my brother-in-law, Brian Gourley. He proposed that I contact Ms. Irena Kuna, Manager of Corporate Sales, Far West, manufacturers of Gortex outdoor clothing. She, too, was impressed and interested in our upcoming voyage and kindly sponsored us by providing each of us with a warm, waterproof, hi-tech outfit which proved more than adequate under severe weather conditions.

Besides searching for sponsorship, I volunteered to help paint *Dove III*, giving Winston more time to work on her interior and the hundred other smaller projects which required his finishing touch. Since I am a professional signpainter, I decided to embellish *Dove* in true Canadian fashion by painting fourteen 61-centimeter-high maple leaves along the entire length of her hull. Besides the lettering, *Dove III*, a flying white dove, signifying peace, was painted on each side of her shapely bow. When the job was completed, I basked in the warm sunlight and sensed a bond between *Dove* and me.

Having concluded my portion of preparing *Dove* for the journey, it was time to focus on myself. A spare pair of glasses, a doctor's checkup, and a visit to the dentist were in order.

April 11, 1995

Yesterday I had two teeth filled that probably should have been extracted; the bone in which they are housed is infected and gradually rotting away. Besides the cleaning and repairs, the dentist kindly prescribed some antibiotics and painkillers in case the teeth become painfully inflamed during the voyage.

We launched *Dove III* on Monday, October 24, 1994, at Newcastle Marina, Nanaimo. This was a proud and happy moment for Winston Bushnell, now one giant step closer to attaining his dream and sailing through the Northwest Passage. Bill King, an enthusiastic and helpful crusader who promoted our journey locally, had the honor of christening *Dove* by pouring champagne across her bow. (Winston preferred the gentle pouring as opposed to smashing the bottle against her bow which he believed to be an act of violence.) It was a strange sensation to hear the cheering crowd while we posed, glasses lifted high, for a toast to *Dove* and the success of our future voyage. As *Dove* was lowered into the salty, cool waters of Newcastle Channel for the first time, I'm sure Winston and George felt much the same as I—like celebrities.

Before *Dove* was returned to Winston's backyard for a few additional adjustments and alterations, we took her for a sea trial. The day was cold and cloudy with a 15-knot southeasterly blowing as we set sail for Norquay Island, a short distance south of Nanaimo near the little seaside town of Chemainus. Ulrich and Margo, well-known for their world-wide sailing excursions, greeted us at the dock of the six-acre island estate they were caretaking. We had planned to return home the same day, but they enticed us to stay for

dinner and spend the night. I enjoyed listening to everyone's sailing tales and went to bed dreaming about our upcoming adventure. Since *Dove* responded well under sail and motored like a gem, our hopes were high as we headed home the following morning to conclude our preparations.

We relaunched *Dove* on February 27, 1995; in almost nine weeks' time, she would begin what might be her greatest voyage. Time was a crucial element in every aspect of this journey and we were kept busy with our final preparations. As agreed, we each chipped in $400 toward the boat's stores and an additional $1,000 for fuel. I wish that's all the trip cost, but when I tallied up my bill at the conclusion of the voyage, the total came to almost $10,000. I'm amazed at how the money goes—but it goes.

April 22, 1995

Winston seems ecstatic about our fast-approaching departure. I must confess that I feel little or no excitement burning in my veins. Perhaps if I were single I would feel differently, but as my eyes click, snapping tiny memory pictures of Sandra to take on the voyage, I realize that a big part of me will be missing.

March and April flew by quickly, like birds on the wing. With slightly more than a week remaining before we sever *Dove's* umbilical cord from the dock, Winston was still asking, "When are you going to start moving your gear aboard, Len?" I recall thinking, "Don't worry, Winston, I won't chicken out."

To the Tip of Vancouver Island

And so it began. . . the long-awaited journey.

May 8, 1995, 0930, George and I slipped *Dove's* mooring lines and, with Winston at the helm, slowly motored toward our destiny—traversing the legendary Northwest Passage.

The send-off was intense and emotional. I struggled to keep a smiling face, but the idea of not seeing or being near the ones who mean so much got the best of me when I saw tears well up in the eyes of Brandi, my youngest daughter. Hugging her tightly to my chest, I surveyed the surrounding crowd of relatives, friends, and well-wishers. Almost everyone was crying or choking back tears, but not my Sandra; she stood true to her word— no tears. We had already said our good-byes while waiting for Alice's Restaurant to open in the early dawn. I remember standing hand in hand as the bright sun lifted its weary head and being astonished when she said quietly, "You know, this is the first sunrise I've ever seen."

The remainder of the send-off was a blur of shaking hands, hugs and kisses. The last thing I remember is calling to my oldest daughter, Iona, "Good-bye! I love you!" and blowing kisses to Sandra and Brandi as they stood shoulder to shoulder on the bow of someone's boat.

As *Dove* slowly passed my home, *Dreamer II*, I saw my late-as-usual daughter Paula standing with my sister Lorraine and yelling, " I love you, Dad! Good-bye! Good luck!" Later, when all the cheers had died away and Nanaimo was a smudge in the distance, I thought, I wonder if I'll ever see home again?

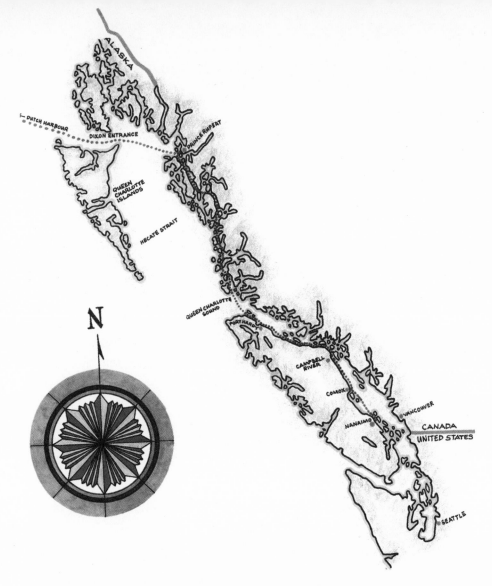

After motoring for nine and a half hours under a heavy, overcast sky, we dropped the hook (anchor) in the calm waters of Comox Harbour.

May 8, 1995

A mere 33 km from home and I feel like a puppy dog that has just been taken away from its mother.

Fortunately, this homesick mood was broken by the arrival of Brent Swain, Winston's friend and *Dove's* designer, whose sloop was anchored only a stone's throw away. This tall, rather unkempt, ruggedly handsome man kept us in a good state of humor. His final remark as he headed out the door was, "Get to bed, Winston! You look like an old fart that's been shot through a keg of nails."

At 0530 the following morning, I was awakened by the fluting vocals of a lone sea eagle, accompanied by the raucous cries of gulls. *Dove* leisurely departed our first anchorage and motored toward Campbell River while an abundance of dark, heavy rain-clouds could be seen on the prowl in the northeastern sky. The slate-grey sea was flat with little or no wind; except for the odd shower, the day was pleasant. We bypassed Campbell River, our intended next stop, in favor of proceeding directly through Seymour Narrows because we arrived at slack time [the period between flood and ebb when the current is not flowing].

Seymour Narrows can be exceedingly dangerous when the current is running at maximum speed; its swift whirlpools and eddies have caused the destruction of many a boat. The infamous Ripple Rock near the entrance, now a mere pebble of itself due to some well-placed sticks of dynamite, no longer poses a threat. *Dove* pushed hastily through the Narrows into Johnstone Strait, and arrived at Vere Cove at the western corner of Thurlow Island.

After spending a calm and comfortable evening at Vere Cove, we hauled up the anchor and once again chugged past the hazardous Ripple Shoal and into Johnstone Strait. The calm morning turned into a blustery afternoon, and for the first time since leaving Nanaimo, we cut loose the sails! Port Hardy, our next destination, beckoned.

As *Dove* drew abeam Malcolm Island on the starboard side, the old Finnish settlement, Sointula, came into view. The little town looked as inviting as it had when I spent a few days there one long-ago summer.

Soon after entering Queen Charlotte Strait, we spotted the flashing green marker on Mastermans Island indicating the entrance to Port Hardy. I had travelled to Port Hardy several times before, but this was the first time by boat.

PORT HARDY

We were tired and it was almost dark, so we secured *Dove* to a log boom for the night. The next morning, we moved her to the Municipal Dock. The small community of Port Hardy has a population of approximately 5,000 people who depend mainly on the logging and fishing industries. It's hard to believe that the once abundant salmon have all but disappeared along the B.C. coast. The government and people put a lot of emphasis on jobs, but what will happen when the sea is exhausted of fish? In Port Hardy, as in Nanaimo—and probably most of the towns situated along the coast—a great many fishing boats tied to the docks have *For Sale* signs attached. Sadly, it is likely that most will never again put to sea in search of salmon, during my lifetime—or ever.

I thoroughly enjoyed the stay at Port Hardy, walking the docks and streets and visiting the small cafes, although there is one cafe I'll never visit again. It shall be left nameless but—beware! While boiling water was poured into the paper cups containing our teabags, Winston and I noticed several small, dark objects bubbling about inside the clear glass container. When we asked what they were, the person pouring the boiling water slyly answered, "Oh, don't worry about that. The water system from the creek is not working properly at the moment, but it won't hurt you." Although the gritty-grots put me off the tea, later I felt even queasier when I strolled by the stream running through the center of town and read the posted sign: *Stink Creek.*

After picking up fresh produce and diesel, we procured a short length of pipe to extend *Dove's* exhaust and stop the soot from blowing into our faces when we steered from the cockpit. George and I each purchased a pair of industrial

ear muffs to shut out the extremely loud engine noise. So far the engine noise wasn't unbearable, but we hated to think what would happen to our hearing when the time came to motor for days on end, especially if we were steering from inside the pilothouse. As it turned out, although I wore ear plugs as well as the ear muffs stuffed with toilet paper, sometimes my ears would ring for three days after the engine was shut off. The clamor of the engine didn't seem to irritate Winston; often he didn't bother to wear ear muffs. However, George and I must have looked comical as we often wore them even while sleeping.

We were ready to leave Port Hardy the next day, but the winds were unfavorable for sailing a direct route from the tip of Vancouver Island to Dutch Harbor in the Aleutian Islands. Also, this being a Friday, a somewhat superstitious Winston said, "It's considered bad luck to leave port on a Friday." Me, I'm not superstitious; no, of course not. However, I always made sure not to whistle at sea. I wonder if that had anything to do with another old superstition: "Don't whistle at sea, 'cause you just might whistle up a storm."

Prince Rupert via the Inside Passage

Saturday, May 13, 0800, we departed Port Hardy. Since the radio still reported strong, unfavorable northwesterly winds at the top end of Vancouver Island, we decided to cruise the well-protected Inside Passage to Prince Rupert rather than take the direct course to Dutch Harbor. George was disappointed; he had been looking forward to the lengthy ocean crossing. But not me, I longed to see the scenic beauty of our own rugged, island-strewn coast.

By ten past ten, *Dove* was abeam the lighthouse on Balaklava Island at Scarlett Point, our last connection to Vancouver Island. This particular area is renowned for whale-watching, but none were to be seen. The wind was blowing 30 knots as *Dove* approached the Storm Islands, which soon fell behind, replaced by Cape Caution looming in the distance off the starboard bow. At this point, the sea was very lumpy due to the large Pacific swells continually rolling across Queen Charlotte Sound. Since *Dove* was pounding directly into the waves, Winston decided to hoist the sails to add a touch more speed and to steady her.

Now in his true element, Winston walked catlike to the bow to help George put up the sails. I was entranced and exhilarated as I steered *Dove* into the wind and through the sparkling blue waters of the Pacific Ocean for the first time. This exquisite feeling of ecstasy was not to last.

I tried not to think about the nausea that slowly but surely was beginning to pervade my being. I tried my best to overcome this contemptible sensation, but finally I had to go below and visit the not-so-beautiful Madame Toilette. Hugging her porcelain-white body, I cooed my innermost thoughts as I lost my innermost contents. I felt almost instantaneous relief and, before the seasickness could take hold again, *Dove* was motoring through the calm waters on the lee side of Calvert Island. I was a happy sailor when the anchor was set at 2045 in Safety Cove, Calvert Island.

We left our comfortable nook at 0715 the next morning, our bellies full of toast lathered with peanut butter and jam. About an hour later, some porpoises came into view, the first I'd seen

Scarlett Point lighthouse, Balaklava Island

in the wild. Since there wasn't a hint of wind, the sea was as flat as a mirror and reflected the spectacular scene of playing porpoises. Winston laughed as I stood at the bow frantically trying to video the sleek, smiling animals dipping and diving through *Dove's* frothy wake. Rather than their frolicsome antics, I captured mostly water on my tape, and felt discouraged. Winston said, "Don't worry, we'll see plenty more when we're crossing the Pacific." Regrettably, we did not. The entertaining porpoises had brightened up a typical drizzly West Coast day and our spirits were scarcely dampened when we arrived at Cecelia Island, just off Reid Passage, and dropped

LEM./96

the hook into the clear, cold water of Boat Inlet for the night.

We left Boat Inlet under a puffy popcorn sky with pockets of blue poking through. By mid-afternoon, the blue had overpowered the white and I sat on deck contemplating and basking in the warm sunlight. As *Dove* motored through the charm and grandeur of the Inside Passage, I wrote:

May 15

Although I have quite a lot of time during the day with little to do, it's difficult to put pen to paper

and express my thoughts and feelings because it
is almost impossible to get private time aboard
such a small boat.

It pained me to see mountainsides that had been literally
scalped bare of trees. I wondered about the mentality of people
who log in such a manner; the forest and the creatures that
once lived there have little chance of making a comeback. Can't
the people responsible see past the few short years they exist
on this planet? Greed is such an ugly commodity.

I looked at the mountains carpeted with lush green trees,
        peaks crowned with sparkling diamonds of snow, and
                sensed a passion of strength and patience.
                    A person would need to be as tenacious
                        as the gnarled roots of an old
                            fir tree clinging to a
                            steep rocky mountain-
                            side to endure such a
                            rugged wilderness. As
                            Dove leisurely made her
                            way through the scenic
                            channels of the Inside
                            Passage, I was over-
                            whelmed by the
                            abundance of natural
                            beauty and, full of rapture
                            and wonder, was inspired
                            to write this simple poem.

Len./96

The Mountain

I see you standing there;
the mist like a shroud
hanging over you.
You've stood for a millennium,
surviving storm and fire;
don't cry!
The zigzag cuts will heal
as will your scabs
where men have scraped you to the bone.
I see your waterfalls
cascading to the sea;
cry not!
For whatever raised you from the sea
will once again see you whole and strong.
Fear not, cry not,
for you will heal.

May 15

When we left Nanaimo last Monday, I was upset, but today, as we chug alongside Princess Royal Island approaching Quarry Point on the port side, I'm feeling a lot better. If the winds are howling on the ocean side of the islands as the radio reported, you'd never know it from here. My stomach has been in good condition since leaving the rough waters of Queen Charlotte Sound. However, I expect to become quite seasick during the open ocean crossing from Prince Rupert to Dutch Harbor. Oh well, not a whole lot I can do; just barf and bear it.

During the past few days, several gargantuan, gleaming-white luxury liners on their way to Alaska have passed us as if we were standing still. The people on the decks look as small as inverted exclamation points. We joked, perhaps a little enviously, about what it would be like to sit around the posh bar sipping champagne, walking the promenades, shopping the ship's mall, and dining on exquisite cuisine at the Captain's table. However, I'm sure that, if given the chance, we wouldn't exchange places. Sailing our own boat to our destination was more rewarding than just buying a ticket for a floating hotel.

We planned to tie up at Butedale, an old abandoned cannery, for the night. However, while we were in the midst of securing *Dove* to a piling, the new owners kindly asked us to move along. I guess they didn't want to be held responsible if the dilapidated docks and buildings suddenly collapsed, wrecking the boat and injuring us. We were dismayed at having to leave, especially as we had been looking forward to exploring the many run-down

buildings. But shortly after leaving Butedale, our disappoint-
ment was lifted by the sight of several spectacular waterfalls
cascading directly into the sea just off the port side.

Having bypassed Butedale, our destination for the night was
Bishop Cove, about 12 km farther north. Daylight
was fast disappearing when we arrived after
having motored a total of 16 hours for the day.
We were three tired sailors when, at 2230
hours, the hook
splashed into
the darkness
between

what looked like a large fishing boat and what sounded like a thunderous waterfall.

The stars and masthead lights dancing on the ripples of the bay were soon replaced by the morning sun winking through the clouds. The fishing boat was gone before I had a chance to poke my head out the door and survey our surroundings. Bishop Cove couldn't have been more beautiful. A semi-transparent, bluish

Butedale

mist hung over the verdant mountains which wrapped around the cove and reached for the heavens. The waterfall was not as large as it had sounded in the dark, but the blue waves lapping against the craggy shore more than made up for it. Although swinging gently on the hook in this scenic paradise was relaxing and mesmerizing, Winston decided to motor *Dove* to a small dock that jutted out from a trail that disappeared into the thick forest. He said the trail led to a natural hot spring.

As soon as we tied *Dove* to the dock, Winston, George and I—towels, soap and beers in hand—headed for the hot spring to enjoy a relaxing bath. The narrow, winding sun-dappled trail, with occasional cedar-planked walkway, led to a small bridge over a wee stream, and a little stone shack nestled beneath the giant bows of an old cedar tree growing near the beach. Inside the hut was a crystal-clear pool of water about 1-1/2 meters deep. The water had no annoying sulfur smell; to sit and relax in this natural hot bath was most luxurious.

We enjoyed ourselves immensely, splashing about *au naturel*,

Bishop Bay hot spring

sipping cool beers and reading the graffiti written on almost every available surface including the rafters. A couple of quotations caught my eye: "F.V. Miss Rachel, '94—it's not that life's too short, it's just that dead is toooo long! great tub!" and "I saw Elvis in the hot tub." Along with our names, *Dove III* was added to the endless list of arrivals.

During the day, *Vector*, a Canadian Ocean and Sciences vessel, anchored just outside the cove. After dinner, a fellow who worked aboard came over for a short visit. He told us that the ship was used primarily by a group of scientists who were keeping a continual update on the conditions of the sea and its creatures. Sadly, his news was not encouraging.

It seems that the harbour of Vancouver, which the government claimed was unpolluted, is just the opposite. When the scientists handled the soil, the skin on their fingers was eaten away; when handled with gloves, they in turn were eaten away. Another place that is regularly studied and analyzed is the severely-contaminated Kitimat region. The clams are diseased so that a person can crush their shells with bare hands. Somewhat disillusioned and angered by what he had told us, I wrote:

May 16

The consensus I've heard so far is that the ecological status of our coast is dire. If the coast, or for that matter, the whole planet, is to be restored and treated with the deep respect which it deserves, the "I could give a shit!" attitude must be halted. Governments and big business—the whole population—must be held accountable for their actions. This frenzy of greed has got to end;

this insatiable gluttony to have and get more and more must stop!

Although the news I heard during our journey at Bishop Cove and elsewhere was disheartening, this short stop was one of the happiest interludes I experienced during the entire voyage. If I could go back to any of the places we visited, Bishop Cove would be my choice. Just imagine, it's in my own backyard!

After leaving the cove, *Dove* encountered squall after squall for the next 40 km. This is typical west coast weather for this time of year. I particularly enjoyed one of my shifts at the tiller, working *Dove* through a fairly strong current. Not that it was dangerous, it just demanded more creative steering. However, Winston had his work cut out for him later on when we needed to locate and navigate the somewhat treacherous entrance to Baker Inlet. He deftly maneuvered *Dove* through the brisk current that ran between the rocks and the moss-laden trees growing on either side of the extremely narrow passage that eventually opened into a spacious anchorage surrounded by high snow-capped mountains.

Baker Inlet, although secluded and serene, was soon disturbed by the throbbing noise of a fishing boat that stopped a short distance away while the crew checked one of the many prawn traps suspended below the surface by large fluorescent red floats. The skipper may have been a poacher, because suddenly he spun the boat in a frothy circle and sped away. Perhaps he thought *Dove* was an official government vessel because of the large hydrography logo displayed on the wheelhouse and all the maple leaves painted along her hull. We laughed at our suspicions and enjoyed the peace of this last Inside Passage anchorage before reaching Prince Rupert.

PRINCE RUPERT

We arrived at Prince Rupert the following afternoon, May 18, exactly ten days after leaving Nanaimo. The weather was sunny and blustery. Docking *Dove* at the Prince Rupert Rowing and Yachting facility proved a touch difficult, but nothing we couldn't handle. Once secured, we made our way to the office to insure that the slip wasn't reserved and to inquire about the daily cost of moorage. It turned out that the slip was reserved; however, after paying $19.26 for a day's moorage, the manager directed us to a spot closer to shore which, as it turned out, was a whole lot more comfortable.

What does one do while at port? Why, check out other boats, of course. Near the end of the long metal gangplank which attaches the docks to the land, I noticed a happy-looking little 6- or 7-meter catamaran painted an unusual bright lime green and purple. A rapidly-spinning wind vane attached to the stern looked like a child's windmill or a whirligig. The little boat seemed like something out of fantasy or a fairy tale. I imagined the people who sailed this little vessel as miniature and congenial. The tiny boat reminded me of Sandra, who hails from the Isle of Man in the Irish Sea. She often talks about the wee folk or fairies living and lurking about the bridges and streams of that fair isle. I thought that this little catamaran would feel right at home tied to a dock at the Isle of Man.

Prince Rupert, "the city of rainbows," is the port of call for many cruise ships, foreign freighters, and B.C. Ferries, as well as the terminus for VIA Railway. It is noted for being the third deepest harbour in the world, with tides rising as high as 11 meters. While we fueled *Dove* from one of several waterfront gas facilities, I peered over the edge of the dock. It was strange to see *Dove* tied so far below, the tip of her mast not quite reaching the edge of the platform where I stood.

This was my third brief visit to Prince Rupert, twice by motorcycle and now by boat. Although famed for its heavy rainfall, I was blessed on each visit with clear and sunny skies. I spent little time sightseeing; however, just before leaving, we managed to treat ourselves to a burger at Smiles Seafood Cafe, established 1934. The platters loaded with burgers and fries were served by a good-looking young waitress named Brandy. Of course, she reminded me of my daughter Brandi and home. I still felt a wee bit homesick.

To save the cost of another day's moorage fee, we motored *Dove* about an hour's distance from Prince Rupert to a little bay just off De Stein Point where we spent a lazy day soaking up the sun's rays. We would have preferred to keep on going toward Dixon Entrance, "the doorway to the North Pacific," but it was Friday. "Bad luck to leave port on a Friday."

Smiles Seafood Cafe, Prince Rupert

As *Dove* swung gently on her anchor in the lightly-rippled cove, I rested languorously amid the cushy sail bags at the bow of the boat and enjoyed the warmth of the afternoon. A tale came to mind that my father once told me about his well-to-do, and eccentric brother, Will, who had once lived in Prince Rupert.

My uncle had bought a brand-new automobile that he apparently didn't know how to drive, so he set it up on blocks inside the garage. Whenever the urge overpowered him, he would fire up the engine, and with the back wheels furiously rotating in mid-air, imagine himself motoring down any road he desired. Another quirk of Uncle Will's was the attitude he took toward his two huge Russian wolfhounds. He would point to one of the walls inside the house and yell, "Rats!" For some reason, he would be immensely delighted when the dogs viciously attacked the walls and tore great gaping holes in them. Besides the wolfhounds, Uncle Will lived with a much younger woman. When he died somewhat mysteriously, leaving everything to her, I heard the word "poison" mentioned on more than one occasion. My father and Uncle Will have long since passed on, but it's memories such as these that warm the heart when there is little to do except wait for tomorrow.

I would have enjoyed lingering longer at Prince Rupert, but adventure beckoned. I looked ahead keenly to the next leg of the voyage—the crossing of the North Pacific Ocean to the Aleutian Islands.

Prince Rupert to the Aleutian Islands

I awoke early Saturday morning from a rather fitful sleep; at 0550, we departed De Stein Point and headed for Dixon Entrance.

May 20, 1220 hours

The weather is beautiful. Winston is at the helm while George snoozes below. In the distance, the Queen Charlotte Islands are barely visible except for the prominence of Tow Hill that rises alongside the Helein River. I once spent a week camped at its base. Who would have thought, when I sat on the beach looking dreamily toward the sea and the distant Alaskan panhandle, that one day I would be on a small sailboat looking back to where I once camped.

Around four in the afternoon, we came across what at first looked like a giant log. We hoped it was a whale floating on the surface of the sea, and when the animal began to cut across Dove's bow, not six meters away, our hopes were answered. This was the first of these magnificent denizens of the sea that we saw on our journey, but not the last. I really wanted to capture the whale on tape, but before I could grab the video camera, the whale blasted a geyser of air and water from its blowhole and slipped beneath the sea. For a long time I stood on the deck and stared in its direction, hypnotized.

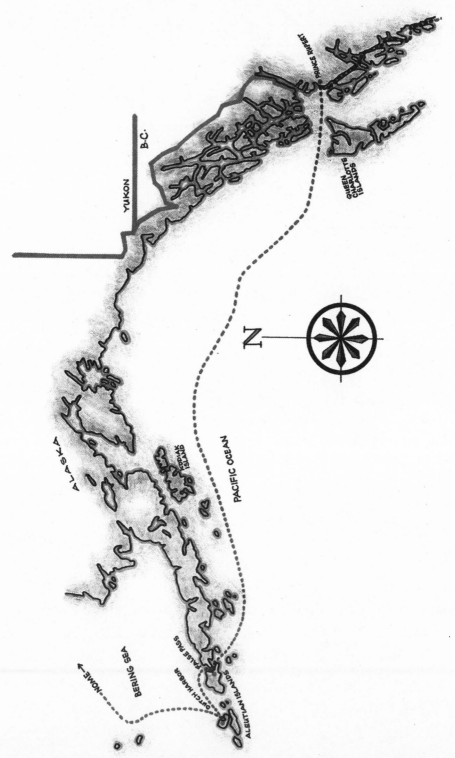

YUKON

B.C.

PRINCE RUPERT

QUEEN CHARLOTTE ISLANDS

N

ALASKA

KODIAK ISLAND

PACIFIC OCEAN

BERING SEA

NOME

ALEUTIAN ISLANDS

FALSE PASS

DUTCH HARBOR

46

May 20

To be so close—to see a whale from such a small, slow-moving craft as *Dove III*—is an awesome experience and I feel blessed to have witnessed such an occurrence.

Sunday, May 21, 1015 hours

The Charlottes have long since slid below the horizon; except for the Alaskan panhandle, there is nothing to see.

Ten days would pass before we again sighted land.

I remember looking eastward for the longest time; the earth as I knew it had completely disappeared. In its place, as far as the eye could see in every direction, was water—water and sky. As long as land is visible, there seems to be a place to go, a direction, a connection, a sense of stability and belonging. However, with only water in view, I felt like an astronaut gazing out of a spaceship's porthole, realizing that if disaster should occur, not even the slightest possibility of walking home existed. Stepping into the water would be almost the same as stepping into outer space—little or no chance for survival.

We took turns at the helm, two hours on and four off. As the journey progressed, we found this was a satisfactory arrangement although I'm sure that Winston and George, like me, would have preferred at times to be at the helm for longer stretches because it helped pass the time more quickly.

On Monday, a westerly began to blow, unfortunately right on *Dove's* nose. In an attempt to conserve fuel and hopefully make a little headway, we raised the sails. *Dove* sailed slowly northward at about 1-1/2 knots with "Pedro"—Winston's pet name for the self-steering device—at the helm. While waiting for a favorable wind change, we did what we liked best—relaxed. Relaxation took the form of reading, snoozing, writing letters or, in my case, keeping a journal. Although *Dove* was cruising along under her own power, we still took turns checking the course and sea conditions and keeping a lookout for any hazards on the horizon.

Since *Dove* was sailing northwards and drifting backwards toward Dixon Entrance, Winston cranked on the engine and headed west in hope of finding a more favorable wind. A 15- to 20-knot southwesterly would have been ideal. As luck would have it, we found the southwesterly. The wind approached as quietly and stealthily as a cat, but the gentle ripples of the sea soon turned into frothing whitecaps. When the wind velocity reached 35 knots or more, I was introduced to the full-blown, howling temper of a North Pacific gale.

For three days, she blew a gale which kept the three of us very busy. The ocean was extremely lumpy and sleep was almost impossible, as was keeping one's footing, cooking, and going to the head (toilet).

One afternoon, as I attempted to prepare dinner, I earned myself a new nickname. Just as I slid the propane stove from its secured slot above the sink and was about to attach it to the gimbals, *Dove* was struck broadside by a powerful wave. I can still see their eyes pop and jaws drop as I gingerly stepped backward and forward, backward and forward, desperately trying to retain my balance and not rip the cord out of the stove, thereby spraying the cabin with its explosive and flammable contents. Winston and George christened me "two-step Lenny."

Going to the toilet was another creative test of agility.

Once, while going to the toilet, I suddenly became airborne. I quickly learned to hold on tightly to the seat and since it didn't break loose, I was okay. However, a word of caution: Watch out for your fingers. If you come down too hard, you could get them pinched.

In truth, I'm not much of a sailor, but I tried to do everything to the best of my abilities. Rod, the fellow who lived aboard *Dreamer II* when I bought her, told me, "Boats are a never-ending learning experience." And so it was aboard *Dove III*; I was learning and, so far, no one had complained. We all had easy-going natures and a similar sense of humor; and you can't knock common sense and experience. We had to be careful about how we reacted to avoid possible hard feelings.

During my shifts at the helm, I derived much delight from three gulls who had been following us faithfully ever since the Alaskan panhandle dipped beyond the horizon. It seemed as if each gull represented one of us. One thing was certain—their presence made for good company. I enjoyed hours of pleasure watching them dip, glide and skim over the whitecaps and between stormy troughs. Just when I thought they had abandoned us, there they would be, floating on the choppy crest of a wave, waiting to rejoin our adventure.

Saturday, May 27, 1245 hours
Position fix: N 56°08' x W 148°10'; 389 kilometers to Dutch Harbor. The gale blew itself out during the night; the sea, once again, was tame and enjoyable.

(Up to this point, it was difficult to get any sleep, which my journal entries verify:

May 24:

Sea was quite rough; slept very little.

May 25:

Boat is rough; hard to sleep, if slept at all.

May 26:

Bumpy, ugly day; gale force winds; no sleep.

Although feeling queasy at times, amazingly I never really got seasick during the entire North Pacific crossing. However, at one point during the three-day gale, I must have been hallucinating due to lack of sleep, because one journal entry reads:

May 28

While at the helm yesterday, just as the sun was setting, I found the sea rather erotic. Its shiny, undulating movements were like the slow gyrations of a sexy belly dancer wearing a translucent gown covered with shimmering rhinestones. The ocean danced teasingly and tirelessly for about an hour until the approaching dark clouds brought the curtain down.

Life aboard *Dove III* was probably much like that on any small sailing vessel crossing an ocean—for the most part, monotonous. Since you couldn't walk much, most of our spare time was spent lying down. Besides steering the boat, we

Aleutian Islands

had small chores to tend to such as changing sail, cooking, doing dishes, filling the fuel tanks, and general maintenance.

Changing sail and cooking during a good blow are rather similar. You have to be sure of foot and deft of hand in both instances. The difference is, if the cooking doesn't fare too well, you could wind up wearing breakfast; if changing sail doesn't go well, the bloody sea could have you for breakfast. Neither is appealing.

As *Dove* slowly crossed the North Pacific, I almost giggled out loud one day as I thought, the ocean is like a sleeping giant and I feel like a toddler crawling across its heaving chest. What if the giant should wake? If it is in good humor and perhaps a little playful, it may give me a wee tickle, but if its mood is angry . . . beware!

The ocean is a marvelous wonder that affected me profoundly. Thankfully, the sea does not have an ego. I admire its simple beauty, ceaseless motion and awesome vastness, but I fear its ominous undercurrent.

One night, while steering *Dove* through an ebony sea beneath a slate-grey sky, I thought about the ones I love who are so far away. My memories shone brightly and gaily like the phosphorescent spray dancing in *Dove's* wake. As cold and alien as the

surrounding ocean seemed, a feeling of warmth overcame me as I realized that to love and be loved is what really matters.

Monday, May 29

Still 250 km to Dutch Harbor. Little or no wind; what there is blows directly on the nose. We need a favorable wind as our fuel is getting seriously low. Winston thinks there is enough remaining for about 150 kilometers.

When I awoke on the morning of May 31, we were approximately 94 km from Dutch Harbor. The sea was the color of liquid lead with ripples of shiny silver that shimmered with the constant rhythm of the slow, undulating rollers. Beneath the dark and ominous clouds stood the long-awaited Aleutian Islands, largest archipelago in the world. Land ho!

During my night shift, *Dove* came across about a dozen whales, their phosphorescent trails glowing like landing lights awaiting a jumbo jet. Being alongside one of these huge beings in the dark can be a little unnerving. However, we didn't bother them and, fortunately, they didn't bother us.

June 1, Thursday, 0800: I awoke to my first real glimpse of the Aleutian Islands as Winston slowly motored *Dove* through Ikatan Bay toward Whirl Point inside Isanotski Strait. The chart showed a cannery on the other side of the narrows and we hoped it wasn't abandoned like the one at Butedale because our fuel tanks were almost completely dry. The entrance looked bleak and inhospitable, but once through the pass, a beautiful bay and the docks of False Pass, Alaska, awaited our arrival.

FALSE PASS

False Pass has a population of only 99, including 22 children. While meandering along the boardwalks of this tiny community on Unimak Island (the first of over 70 Aleutian Islands), I wondered what sort of person would choose to live in such a bleak, desolate and remote area of the world. I tried to imagine myself as one of the 99 inhabitants. As strange as it may seem, melding into such an environment and society actually seemed possible. However, when speculating on how I would earn a living, I failed miserably.

During our extremely short but delightful stay at False Pass, we were befriended by the wholesome and devout Jacobson family: Jake, the community overseer, his wife Heidi, three young daughters, and a seventeen-year-old foster son. Heidi prepared a delicious meal for us of moose chili, macaroni, and homemade, plate-moppin' bread. Before digging in, we joined hands and bowed our heads while Jake gave thanks and asked safe journey

False Pass

for the three tired strangers who had landed at his doorstep. Sitting there, with the Alaskan sun streaming through the kitchen windows, I felt a bond of friendship as we all said, "Amen."

We sat around the large kitchen table, enjoying a good cup of Earl Grey tea, while Jake and Heidi told us that they might return to California. They felt the move would give their children the chance to enhance their education and be part of a larger society with more opportunities available. They were concerned about the prevalence of violent crimes, drugs and pollution.

Jake told us that the children of False Pass had a drug problem, which surprised me. I thought that such a small community—there's only one general store—would be safe from petty drug dealers. Hard to believe that the evil of drugs had reached this far. I guessed the drugs were brought in by an occasional fishing boat.

False Pass

Jake also mentioned the poor taste of California water compared to that of False Pass, "the best-tasting drinking water in the world." (He had no argument from me on that point; the drinking water aboard Dove tasted horrible.)

I was relieved to hear that, despite the drug problem, the Jacobsons were leaning toward staying in False Pass rather than moving to "sunny California."

Just before we left, Jake and two of his daughters clambered aboard Dove for the nickel tour. I got the impression he was amazed at how little room we had, but the girls felt differently. They took great delight playing pirates and wanted to go for a sail. One said, "When I grow up, I'm going to live on a sailboat and have a horse on it, too." I had to laugh when she asked, "Do you think there's room here for a horse?" Thank you, Jake, Heidi and family, for our warm and generous introduction to Alaskan hospitality.

We departed False Pass at four the same afternoon, following a never-ending series of range markers that directed us through the labyrinth of Bechevin Bay sandbars to the Bering Sea. When Dove finally entered the placid, glacial-green sea, I had a feeling that the sense of tranquillity could be stormily interrupted at any moment. After all, the Aleutian Islands, which point westward like a finger from the fist of Alaska, are noted for their volcanic activity, and the Bering Sea is equally renowned for its stormy personality.

June 1, 2245 hours
65 kilometers to Dutch Harbor—great day.
Sunny and warm; no wind.

1,800 kilometers from home. Dutch Harbor would soon be more than just a dot on a chart; it would become a reality, as would the many dots yet to come. Winston had told us so much about this little port that I eagerly looked forward to our visit.

DUTCH HARBOR

June 2, 1700 hours, we arrived at Dutch Harbor, the crossroads of the Aleutian Islands. As well as the name of the harbour, Dutch Harbor is also the name for the part of the city located on Amaknak Island. The other part of the city is on Unalaska Island. In 1980, a bridge was built to connect the split city of Unalaska.

> The waters of Dutch Harbor are ice-free year round
> and the spit provides a sheltered anchorage for
> vessles [sic] from the storms of the North Pacific and
> Bering Sea.
> **—From the journal of John Ledyard, an American
> who sailed with Captain Cook in 1778.**

Winston motored *Dove* to what is known as the "small boat harbor" facility, located at the farthest corner of Dutch Harbor. Directly across, the formidable 130-meter Bunker Hill looks down with furrowed brow, while behind it rises the active volcano, Mount Makushin, pumping clouds of steam.

Dove was soon boarded by two authoritative-looking Customs agents wearing distinctive, gold badges. Most people who wear uniforms intimidate me. However, the two Customs officers proved to be amiable and helpful while asking pertinent questions about our arrival and future destination. They stamped our passports, a real treat for me as this was my first passport. After their departure, we quickly scrambled ashore in search of the Post Office, always a highlight upon arrival at the various ports during our journey. Unfortunately, the Post Office was closed until Monday. Although somewhat discouraged and disheartened, all wasn't lost as I could still phone home.

Talking to Sandra was wonderful; almost like being home. Although the conversation was mostly on the happy side, I felt that she sounded a little depressed. I thought, I hope she holds herself together until my return. I'd feel badly if something happened to her, especially since she put so much effort and money into helping to make this voyage possible. She said she had bought a Yorkshire terrier named Cricket to give her and Misty, our other little dog, more company. Replaced by a dog, I thought. Sandra asked if I was upset about having another dog on board. How could I be? If the puppy would help keep her happy, I was all for it.

When a person leaves home to travel, he may fail to imagine the effect his leaving could have on the home front. The one who stays home says, "Go ahead, have a good time; I'll be fine until you return." However, once the two people are separated and realize they are alone, both parties can become quite despondent.

The next day, George and I met a Finnish couple who were in the process of sailing around the world. They had been at Dutch Harbor for some time, waiting for parts in order to repair their self-steering system. We were invited aboard their deluxe sailboat which included—much to our surprise—a sauna! Sitting at the spacious galley table, enjoying a drink and swapping sailing sagas, I began to experience a warm, light-headed sensation. Knowing what would happen if I didn't reach fresh air immediately, I quickly made an excuse for leaving, but no sooner did I stand than I fainted and fell to the floor.

Consciousness came back slowly and I wondered what all the people were doing in my dream. As I became more aware of my surroundings, I was relieved to find I hadn't wet myself, something that had occurred on another such occasion, in a very public place, some years earlier. While reassuring everyone, especially a very concerned George, I collapsed once again. Finally, with George's assistance, I made it outside and was almost instantly revived by the fresh air.

I've experienced a few such fainting episodes during my lifetime, caused mainly by severe pain or fatigue. In this case, I suspect that being overtired was the cause. Fortunately, this never occurred again during our trip. On returning to *Dove*, Winston mixed up a hearty shot of rum in a glass of Neo-citron that totally knocked me out. Boy, did I sleep!

Sunday, June 4

Happy Birthday, Iona (eldest daughter). I wrote letters all day. The weather has been nice, but I guess there is a real howl of a wind coming out of the northeast across the Bering Sea, the direction we want to go.

Dutch Harbor, which depends primarily on the fishing industry, is an extremely busy place. Many of the 4,500 people living here are employed by a large fishing plant known as Unisea. Like many other large corporations in small communities, Unisea supplies its employees with accommodations and food. However, from what I heard, some of the workers still had to hold down two full-time jobs in order to survive because rent and food were very expensive. Talk about an "I owe my soul to the company store" town—this was it.

I learned that a large degree of animosity existed between the Aleuts (native Aleutians) and the Americans. At one time, the Aleuts inhabited most of the Aleutian Islands, but now call only a few of them home. I can't blame the Aleuts for their bitterness, as the word they use to describe their homeland is "ounalashka," the beautiful land. As I explored the streets and countryside, I noticed a lot of landscaping in progress that was drastically changing the lay of the land. I could scarce believe my eyes as I watched a large, rocky hill actually being flattened by what looked like a giant jackhammer. In Dutch Harbor, like most places caught in the strangling grip of commercialism for survival, desecration of the land is not a major concern.

I met only two Aleuts, or people I believed were Aleuts, during our stay. One, an elderly man strolling along the beach, told me about a large tidal wave which sucked all the water out to sea. I was amazed to learn it had caused little damage. The other person I met who looked like a native Aleut was fishing on the beach. After casting his line in hopes of a catch, he said with a slight grin, "A lot of tourists take my picture and I have been in several brochures, but I'm not an Aleut. I'm from the Philippines." We both had a good laugh about this.

During the Second World War, the Japanese invaded the Aleutian Islands and actually attacked Dutch Harbor. Many military remnants can still be seen; for example, caved-in bunkers, abandoned concrete machine-gun nests, and a submarine docking facility now operating as the Walashek Shipyard. The Aleutian Campaign, "The One-Thousand-Mile War," was the first battle to be fought on American soil since the Civil War.

I also learned, to my dismay, that the Alaskan king crab, as well as many other marketable inhabitants of the surrounding seas, are on a steep decline. Since commercial fishing is becoming less viable, the so-called fishing magnates, with eyes larger than their bellies, now look toward the attractions of sport fishing and tourism. Plans are in place to downsize the larger fishing vessels in favor of smaller charter boats in order to lure the affluent tourists to fish for whatever remains, and to show them the rapidly-vanishing whales, walruses, sea otters, etc.

Being an artist and a romantic at heart, perhaps I see the negative aspects more than the positive, but the reality of the Aleutian Islands and Dutch Harbor wasn't quite what I expected. I had envisioned lofty, snow-capped mountains and soaring, proud, "land of the free" eagles. Instead, the mountains were being pulverized while the eagles dined on fish guts. I wish I had kinder things to say, because my stay was enjoyable and the people hospitable.

Five days after arriving at Dutch Harbor, we were still waiting for the winds to die down and shift to a more favorable direction. For one who usually enjoys his time ashore exploring the sights and meeting the people, I was unusually impatient about leaving, although the dock people had been more than generous and entertaining. Take, for example, Chris Skelley and his girlfriend, Rebecca Goodridge, who lived aboard a well-weathered houseboat he had built to avoid the high rents.

Chris has vivid blue eyes and a head of almost pure-white, thick, curly hair with matching mustache. With the articulation and excitement of a small boy, he is a man with a dream. He wanted to build a 16-meter catamaran, and the plans were tacked to the rough-hewn center beam of the houseboat. His eyes twinkled with delight as he said, "I like it here at Dutch Harbor, but after eight years of fishing the ice-cold waters of the Bering Sea, it's time to go where a heater isn't needed."

His girlfriend, Rebecca, a cheerful, down-to-earth, attractive redhead, was a different personality. We had some good discussions, especially about the book she was writing on King Arthur and Guinevere. I told her some people believe that they were married at Peel Castle on the Isle of Man and she should write my wife for more information, which she did. Rebecca was an excellent conversationalist and a great cook. The evening before we left, she prepared a delicious feast of Alaskan king crab, the first I'd ever eaten.

Another dockside character I met was a big man named Ernie, or "Pacer," as Winston aptly named him. For hours on end, he would pace the dock in front of his small aluminum boat moored directly across from *Dove*. You'd swear he had a steam engine for a heart, for great clouds of smoke billowed about him as he trod. Ernie admitted to smoking five packs of cigarettes a day, probably the reason he coughed and wheezed so much.

grave yard

His continual pacing and constantly turned-on radio seemed to irritate Winston, but I rather got a kick out of him. Perhaps Ernie's incessant walking up and down the dock stemmed from his loneliness.

One cloudy, drizzly afternoon, Ernie and I sat on the dock sipping cold Rainier beer while he told me of the recent loss of his family which had consisted of two large dogs. They had been his constant companions for the past 16 and 18 years. Pointing to a craggy bluff overlooking the harbour a stone's throw away, he said, "I buried them there." His Scandinavian voice almost broke as he spoke. "I really miss them," he said. "They were like my kids . . . and sometimes . . . I still cry when I think about them."

A vision of smoke like a halo surrounding a hang-dog face with large ears and bloodshot eyes comes to my mind and my heart goes out to Ernie. At age 62, he is still a strong man who fits his size 12 boots well. I wrote in my journal:

> He paces and waits for his dream to become a reality; the dream of a prospector—gold. I don't know what you have done in your lifetime, Ernie, but I have seen a glint of gold in your heart. Buff it up—make it shine—for the gold within you is worth more than you'll ever find in the bowels of the earth or along some winding creek bank. Let it shine, Ernie, and you'll never be lonely again.

To conserve our financial resources, we left the dock and anchored *Dove* a short distance away in Iliuliuk Bay.

June 9

Damp, damp, damp—everything is damp. No matter what I touch, the feel of clamminess abounds. As I write, I've had to cover my legs with a small sheet of plastic to deter a persistent drip caused by condensation on the wheelhouse windows. Sweat, sweat, sweat; drip, drip, drip; like the ticking of a clock, the monotony of dampness is slowly seeping into my bones.

Holy Ascension Cathedral

The people of Dutch Harbor have a saying: "If you don't like the weather, wait five minutes and it'll change." I noticed quite a bit of truth in this adage; however, on this particular day, it never changed, but rained all day. Unfortunately, I hadn't been keeping a close watch on the drips and some of them managed to seep between the pages of my journal which was written with a fountain pen and non-waterproof ink. Much to my horror, many of the words and sentences ran. Although the pages looked messy, I was still able to make them readable.

The next day, George, Winston and I walked over to Unalaska Island for

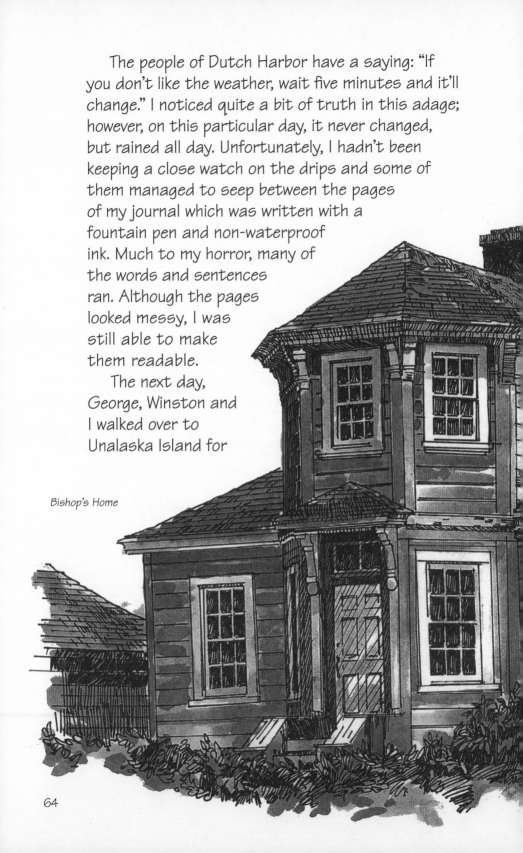

Bishop's Home

a last bit of sightseeing and to take some photographs of the Holy Ascension Cathedral, a Russian Orthodox church erected in 1824.

The old church and the nearby Bishop's home were badly run down and were being restored. Both buildings are on the "top ten" list of the "most endangered historical landmarks in the United States."

On the following morning, June 10, we motored out of Iliuliuk Bay past the narrow spit of Dutch Harbor toward the Bering Sea. As the Holy Ascension Cathedral faded behind *Dove's* wake, I noted towering Mount Makushin, its volcanic steam hard to distinguish from the white, billowy clouds hovering in the distance. I felt a pang of sadness as the little town of Dutch Harbor slowly disappeared from view.

Len./96

Across the Bering Sea to Nome

June 10

Welcome to the Bering Sea, Len. . . two-meter seas; wind out of the north, right on the nose; seasick. 1745 hours: vomited.

No wonder I felt a little sad about leaving Dutch Harbor; who enjoys being sick?

Sunday, June 11

Three-to-six-meter seas; very lumpy as we motored hard into the wind. Seasick; vomited again. Have slept about one and a half hours in the past 24. For most of the day we hove to [to reduce sail so a vessel makes little or no headway but merely comes to and falls off by the counter-action of the sails and helm].

At the mercy of the gale and waves, *Dove* slowly drifted toward the American Pribilof Islands.

Monday, June 12

Wind is still blowing about 30 knots. Sea conditions about the same as yesterday; still hove to. George has been more seasick than I, but is still able to do whatever is asked. The sea life agrees with Winston.

The Bering Sea is named after the early Danish explorer, Vitus Bering, who sailed from Siberia with a crew of Russian sailors in search of whatever lands lay to the east. On July 16, 1741, Bering sighted "Alyeska" or what is know today as Alaska. I wonder if Vitus Bering was as boisterous and as much a bully as the Bering Sea is in its treatment of us.

June 13

Gale force winds still blowing. We're about one-third of the distance to Nome, and although we are not sailing in the desired direction, we are still making some headway. With "Pedro" at the helm, the ride is more comfortable. We all managed to get some much-needed sleep and are able to eat a little more substantially.

 I feel almost guilty for lying around so much, but the truth is, it's almost impossible to do anything else because *Dove* is constantly rocking and rolling. Sometimes an occasional wave—about the size of a semi—will smash into the side, almost knocking her over. At one point, when the waves were anywhere from 2-6 meters in height, Winston was worried *Dove* might capsize. When he mentioned this, I was chilled with fear.

I wondered how long the rough weather would last. How long before an unusually large, rogue wave would broadside us? How long could we survive if we were forced to abandon *Dove?* Fortunately, *Dove* was never capsized and the tempestuous weather soon eased.

 Besides being exceedingly rough, the weather was bitterly cold and *Dove's* interior wasn't much better. For the first time on the voyage, Winston decided to fire up the little woodstove located just below the pilothouse floor at the foot of his bunk. After much fuss, the presto log finally caught fire.

However, the wind flowed off the mainsail and gusted down the chimney; continual blasts of air caused the fire to smolder and filled the cabin with clouds of black smoke. Failing to obtain a satisfactory fire, a teary-eyed Winston adjusted the chimney, but huge billows of dark grey smoke filled the boat from floor to ceiling. Winston finally had to admit defeat.

To ensure that the fire was out, Winston poured water on it which, of course, doubled the density of the smoke. Winston was hidden in the smoke, but I could hear him muttering and I began to laugh. Hearing me, a not-too-amused Winston sputtered, "Quit laughing, Len!" But for the life of me, I couldn't stop.

When Winston finally emerged from below and saw me laughing, he began to laugh, too. Tears streaming down our cheeks, we escaped to the fresh air of the cockpit to wait for the smoke to dissipate. To this day, I don't know how George stood it. Since he couldn't be seen for the smoke, I can only guess that he kept himself totally covered in his sleeping bag throughout the ordeal.

After the smoke had cleared, Winston plotted a course to Nunivak Island. The plan was to sail through Etolin Strait which separated the island from the Alaska mainland, continue along the coastline, and then cross the wide expanse of Norton Sound to Nome.

Two days later, we arrived at Nunivak Island. After motoring past some Eskimo hunters' white tents, glowing on the dark shoreline, we dropped anchor at 0230 hours in a quiet little bay. I was amazed at how light it still was. After the uncomfortable harshness of the Bering Sea, the gentle sway of Dove on her hook made me feel like a babe being rocked to sleep in the arms of an angel.

We left our placid anchorage at 1120 Friday and sailed in search of Mekoryuk, a small Eskimo village on the northern shore of the island just beyond Cape Etolin. Winston figured the village would be a good place to do a little engine maintenance.

As I steered *Dove* along the northeastern shore of the tundra-covered island, I noticed a couple of buildings in the distance with two very small islands just offshore. I thought the buildings must be part of the village and that because of the scale of the chart, the tiny islands were not shown. I wasn't sure what to do: go between the shore and the islands or go around them. Although there seemed to be enough water between the shore and the islands, I didn't know the depth. As the islands drew dangerously near, I grew nervous and summoned a sleeping Winston. After a quick look, he exclaimed excitedly: "Turn 'er hard and take 'er around the islands."

I carried out Winston's order immediately, but as I steered *Dove* around the farthest island with what we thought was a safe margin, she suddenly hit a rock with a terrible crunching noise, then bounced off into water that luckily was two meters deep. My heart almost stopped when *Dove* struck. Later, when *Dove* was motoring safely through deeper water, Winston quietly said, "Good thing you didn't take 'er between the island and the shore, Len. You probably would have put us high and dry."

After *Dove's* close call, nearly running aground, Winston figured the motor maintenance could wait until our arrival at Nome. Later the same day, just before dark, I wrote:

Saturday, June 17

As I enjoyed the spectacular sunset, the vivid pinks of the sky interplaying with the soft greys of the clouds, I imagined that all this splendor was created just for me. Like the sea around me, I was suffused by the heavenly hues. I was overcome with a sensation of complete and utter awe and I felt something like a presence which surrounded me with warmth and love. It was as if the heavens, the earth, and I were one. I wept.

On Saturday, June 25, the silhouette of a tug pulling a barge appeared on a horizon that looked like the edge of the world. As it slid along against the brilliant blue sky, I was inspired to write this poem.

The Sailor's Prayer

I saw a tug just the other day
pulling a barge along the edge of the world.
It was filled with souls that were still unfurled;
they were on their way to their judgment day.
And though the tug seemed to pass me by,
I clasped my hands and I began to cry;
for through the tears I could plainly see
the tug had turned and was coming t'wards me.
So I fell to my knees, and I began to pray.
Oh Lord,
I know at times I've been bad,
sometimes even very bad;
and then again, I've been good,
at times even very good.

But Lord,
to change the bad into good,
in all honesty, if I could,
I'm not sure that I would.
I had a feeling all would be well,
so I opened my eyes and looked out to sea.
In every direction there was naught to see:
no tug, no barge, not a soul fare-thee-well.
Was it a dream, a trick of the eye,
when all I could see was ocean and sky?
As the tears on my face slowly dried,
I realized something deep inside me had died,
so I stayed on my knees, and I continued to pray.
Oh Lord,
I ask not for your forgiveness
for my every weakness;
though a sinner I may be,
this is all I ask of thee.
Please Lord,
remember I'm just me,
a sailor of the sea,
I'm not so strong as thee.

As we approached the port of Nome, Alaska, a heavy fog set in. At times, the mist was so dense it was impossible to see much farther than 6 meters ahead. The strange thing was that if I looked directly upwards, it seemed I could see forever. The GPS (Global Positioning System) was great for determining our position and speed, but hazardous obstacles were another matter. Since *Dove* wasn't equipped with radar, we had to keep a careful watch. When the fog finally lifted, we could clearly see Nome dead ahead, about three-quarters of a kilometer away.

The U.S. Coast Guard's ice breaker, *Storis*, lay at anchor just offshore Nome. We circled around the giant vessel while the exuberant crew yelled greetings and gave us directions for entering the inner harbour behind the Snake River jetty. The entrance was shallow—only one and a half meters deep—and I crossed my fingers as *Dove* slowly entered the harbour. Luckily, she didn't bottom out in the pounding surf, and by 0115, she was secured to the dock. Before crawling into our sleeping bags, we celebrated our crossing of the Bering Sea and safe arrival at Nome with hot double rums.

NOME

My first impression of Nome, as I strolled its dusty streets, was of an old "Wild West" town somehow seriously misplaced. I almost expected to see gun-slinging cowboys sauntering the streets instead of camera-addicted Orientals and elderly blue-haired tourists. Although there were quite a few western-style saloons such as the Golden Nugget Hotel, I wasn't able to mosey in and sashay up to the bar; I couldn't afford a coffee, let alone a beer. (Our budget for the journey fell far short of our requirements.)

A lot of the town looked as though a division of Sherman tanks had rolled through not bothering to use the streets. Many remnants of the Second World War were still visible—numerous, dilapidated quonset huts and long, narrow K.D. (knock-down) buildings put together in prefabricated sections of 1.5 meters. Very little of Nome's Gold Rush, Victorian architecture remains due to the many fires and storms over the years. In 1934, for example, a fire completely destroyed the business section and a large portion of the residential areas surrounding it.

There's a story about how Nome got its name. It is said that the original name came from a fifty-year-old spelling mistake. An officer aboard a British ship noted on a chart that the nearby prominent point of land was unnamed. He wrote, "? name" on the area; when the chart was later recopied, a mapmaker mistook the "a" in "name" for an "o" and christened it "Cape Nome."

This theory is not generally accepted by the locals; they believe the word "Nome" was derived from an Eskimo phrase, "kn-no-me," meaning "I don't know." They figure this reply was used by the Eskimos when asked the name of the area.

In its Gold Rush heyday during the first decade of this century, with an estimated population of 20,000, the place was known as Anvil City. However, the U.S. Post Office insisted on calling the community Nome, after the nearby cape, as Anvil City was too easily confused with the village of Anvik.

Nome still depends on gold as one of its main industries. Of the 40 gold dredges in the area, only one remains operational, the others are abandoned. I managed to explore one of these decaying derelicts located on the outskirts of town. Although this earth-belching, gold-straining dredge would never run again, I could imagine how sophisticated it seemed when compared to the drudgery of gold panning. The Gold Rush boom ended long ago, but each year many gold-panners and prospectors with portable mini-dredges arrive in droves, erecting what is known as "Tent City" along the shores of Nome.

During our short stay in Nome, we met many people. One was Joy, a woman who managed the docks by day and sang professionally by night. Another was the likable Terry Wilson. This burly man, with his infectious laughter, was so interested in building a steel sailboat that he showed up early one morning with a dozen delicious donuts to pump Winston for as much information as he could get about how *Dove* was built. There were others, too, such as the entrepreneur, Chic, who had an import/export business with Russia, and the Norwegian, Ragnar Kvan and his girlfriend, busy sailing around the world while writing articles about their travels. Ragnar actually interviewed the three of us over a six-pack of cold beer with the intention of writing an article for a Norwegian magazine.

One character I met who stands out in my mind was Vic Goldsberry, the proprietor of a small craft store dealing with Eskimo artisans from both Russia and Alaska. He had a wealth of information about the artists and their crafts—most were either personal friends or relatives. While I photographed Vic and various pieces of the artwork for sale, he described each piece in detail, how it was made and by whom. I admired a small, finely-carved and realistic ivory polar bear sitting on its haunches. He

Abandoned gold
dredge, Nome

told me it had been carved in Russia and although its price of $90 seemed reasonable, I couldn't afford it. Vic said that he would like to sell and trade some items from my country, but Canada has a ban on the import of any mammal parts—skins, horns, bones or organs.

Vic had great compassion for the Eskimo people; I got the feeling he was ashamed of the treatment they had received from the American government. When the Americans purchased Alaska from Russia in 1867, Eskimo children were taken from their parents and villages, inducted into the American school system and restrained from speaking their native language. The adults became despondent, many taking to drinking alcohol heavily. As one of the Eskimos told Vic, "What are homes without children?" Segregation was also imposed during the Second World War. Eskimos were not allowed to sit with white people

and were made to enter businesses through the back door. This was a constant embarrassment for the many servicemen who married Eskimo women. What Vic told me was no surprise, as I have read about our own government's lack of respect for the indigenous peoples of Canada.

On leaving Vic's store, Chukota-Alaska, Inc., for the last time, I was surprised and pleased when he presented me with a gift made in Russia. There were small, hand-carved human figures, colorfully-enameled, enclosed in a finely-crafted wooden box that opened to form a checkerboard-type of game. Generosity such as Vic Goldberry's really made my trip worthwhile.

Just as we were about to leave Nome, Winston received notice of a large ice pack floating a little to the north under a dense cover of fog; because of our restricted time frame, we had to press on despite the report. We refueled Dove, stored fresh produce, and topped off the water tanks, and Winston visited Mr. Stolz who was in charge of Nome's weather station. He gave Winston several faxes concerning the ice conditions and a complete set of highly-detailed navigational charts of the Alaskan coast all the way to the Canadian border. What a gift! I doubt that we would have made it through the American side without the aid of those charts.

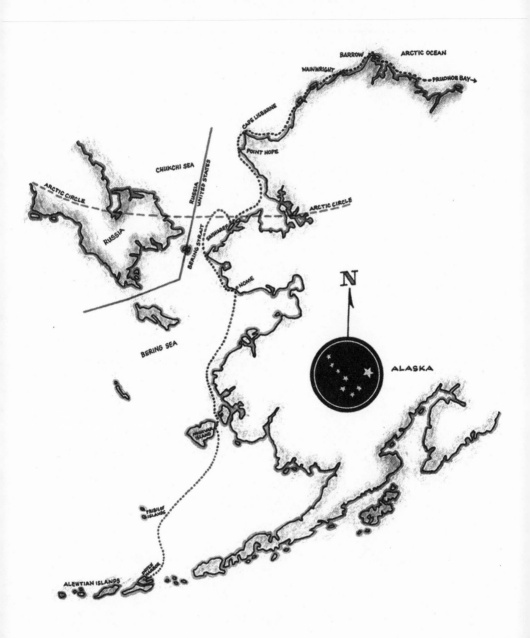

First Encounter with the Ice
Nome to Barrow

Dove departed Nome on Thursday, June 22, at 1040 hours. By four o'clock in the afternoon, we were motoring toward Little Diomede Island (U.S.) and Big Diomede Island (Russia), approximately 50 km distant in the center of the Bering Strait. We had decided against visiting the Russian port of Provideniya because of the political problems running rampant in that country. We bypassed the American Diomede Island because Ragnar Kvan had told us that it was very expensive to arrive by boat. It was a bit disheartening to be so close to Russia and not visit; it was one of the places we had looked forward to seeing from the beginning of our voyage.

Friday, June 23, approximately 1330 hours

Crossed the Arctic Circle. Hooray!! Winston says we are one of the elite to have sailed this far north.

Saturday, June 24, 1700 hours

Ice, ice, ice and more ice! The first we've seen. Pretty scary! Travelling, or should I say, picking our way through the pack ice for the first time was a little unnerving.

Pack ice is the frozen surface of the sea that, as temperatures rise, breaks away from the shore. Pieces of this saltwater ice may be as small as your fist or as large as a football field. Moved by the forces of wind, current and tide, pack ice poses a threat to all vessels, large or small.

Ice floes are chunks of ice that have broken off of icebergs and come in assorted sizes and irregular shapes. Icebergs are giant fragments of glaciers that shatter as they reach the sea. This fresh-water glacial ice can be thousands of years old.

Sunday, June 25, 1207 hours

We are currently backtracking from Point Hope after an unsuccessful attempt to pass through or around many miles of pack ice. Last night, around midnight, we secured Dove to a small ice floe so we could get some sleep after battling the ice all day. The wind- and sea-sculpted ice floes which surround us are as silent as sentries. Upon awakening, we found the ice had tightened its grip and Dove had drifted toward the main ice pack. I had a moment of panic when, still half-awake, I heard Winston exclaim: "We gotta get outta here!"

After a brief difference of opinion between Winston and George as to which course to take, the decision was made by the ice. We are drastically out of our element, I thought. After the last 24-hour encounter with the pack ice, I'm losing some of my confidence in this journey.

SHISHMAREF

After backtracking for over a day through myriad spectacular ice floes, we arrived at the small Eskimo village of Shishmaref, located on the tiny banana-shaped Sarichef Island. The village, in stubborn defiance of the constant wind and pounding surf, clings to the tundra-covered island that rises no higher than

4.5 meters above sea level at its highest point. There is an airstrip on either side of the community, one operational, the other abandoned.

Upon arrival, George and I rowed ashore to check out the possibility of purchasing some fuel. As we climbed the bank of the litter-strewn, sandy beach, a lone Husky tethered to a wooden pole greeted us with a startling wolf-like howl. It was disconcerting when the whole dog population joined in melancholy harmony. As soon as we crossed the soggy, spongy tundra to the weather-beaten shanties set on both sides of the narrow, dusty road, we were met by a short, stout, smiling Eskimo. He reached out his well-tanned hand and said, "Welcome. My name is Bill, I'm the Mayor of Shishmaref."

Bill told us about the people of Shishmaref and their way of life. He said that the main occupation on the island was hunting. This was evident; seals and walruses, their skins pegged for tanning and their meat drying on racks, surrounded the

village. Bill was concerned about housing since the island was becoming over-populated. "It wasn't long ago that only 220 people lived here," he said. "Now the population has expanded to 560; even the kids are having kids." He was also worried about the villagers' welfare since only a few paying jobs existed and the government had drastically cut their funding budget. This seems to be a familiar practice everywhere these days.

After we trudged further into the village, taking care to avoid being run over by a speeding ATV (all-terrain vehicle), we were approached by several Eskimos trying to sell their carvings. Although each small sculpture was intricately carved of bone and inlaid with ivory and baleen, one piece looked much the same as the other because the artists chose the same subject matter over and over. So much for Lenny the Arctic traveller, now I was Lenny the tourist.

Eventually we located the general store and fuel pumps which were unfortunately some distance from the boat. Hauling eight empty fuel containers across the deep, soft tundra to the pumps would not pose a problem, but we weren't looking forward to the return journey. Each container would weigh about 23 kilograms. Fortunately, we learned that there was a truck that would deliver it.

The gas pump read $77 and the clerk asked us for $114. "The computer isn't running properly," he said, "and there's a 4 percent tax charge." Winston objected and the clerk finally settled for $93. We felt ripped off.

As we loaded the fuel containers on the truck to be delivered to the shore, I noticed a small sign on the gas pump that read: "Not legal to tax this fuel." I can't recall the price per liter, but I do know that the farther north we travelled, the more expen-

Toasting King Neptune

sive everything became. Also, the exchange on American currency really hurt the old pocketbook.

We left Shishmaref on June 27 at 1100 hours. The bay was extremely shallow and *Dove* ran aground several times before getting through the entrance to the open sea. I looked back at the grey, weather-beaten shacks huddled together on the shore, each with a howling Husky chained to a post, and thought, the people who live there are hardier than I am.

Because we had had to backtrack, *Dove* again crossed the Arctic Circle not long after we left Shishmaref. And, as tradition dictates, we once again enjoyed toasting Neptune with drams of grog (rum). Perhaps we should have remained near the Arctic Circle, continually crossing back and forth.

Dove was making good time through the Chukchi Sea until the constantly-moving pack ice clutched her in its icy fist. However, we eventually worked her free through the many twisting leads and reached Cape Thompson on June 28 at 1140. While I was preparing some flapper-jacks (pancakes) down below, two aluminum skiffs, each containing three Eskimo hunters, pulled alongside. They were amazed at the size of Dove and how far we had travelled. We talked for some time, mostly about the ice conditions and the prospects of reaching Point Hope. They had killed several seals and asked if we had seen any walruses. George told them he had seen one not too far back in the ice, so that's where they headed.

POINT HOPE
Like a long bony finger, Point Hope juts into the Chukchi Sea for approximately 12.5 km; it is probably not much higher than six meters above sea level. Since the Eskimo village on the point

offered no protection from the onslaught of perilous ice floes in the Chukchi Sea, we bypassed it in favor of Marryatt Inlet.

Not long after *Dove* rounded Point Hope, George, high in the ratlines [lines running horizontally across the shrouds and used as a ladder], spotted the narrow, shallow cut leading into Marryatt Inlet. A weather-worn Eskimo cabin stood like an abandoned World War II guardhouse at the port side of the entrance. Since *Dove* anchored on the other side of the inlet, I never had the opportunity to take a close look at this lonely, forlorn structure. However, I did manage to explore part of the long, narrow peninsula. A great deal of wood had drifted ashore, but not a tree or shrub was to be seen. Since it was either late spring or early summer, an abundance of tiny, beautifully-colored flowers flourished amidst the gravel, sand and patches of tundra. I was amazed to find a familiar flower growing in this barren landscape. It was the persistent, tenacious, determined and defiant bane of lawn-growers everywhere—the dandelion.

As I wandered slowly along the shoreline, I noticed the sparkling white and turquoise hues of the jagged ice in sharp contrast to the dull greys and browns of the smooth, rolling hills and rounded mountain tops. By a small pond, I discovered the splayed tracks of a lone caribou where it must have stopped for a drink. Farther along, some unidentifiable tracks appeared in the loose gravel and I followed them. I felt a cold prickling sensation on the nape of my neck when I realized that the tracks were those of a bear, most likely a polar bear. Not far ahead, glistening white in the sunlight, lay the skeletal remains of what I thought was a walrus, although neither skull nor tusks (a popular medium for Eskimo carvers) were evident. While examining the skeleton, I heard a large splash among the bergs and, my imagination and senses on high-alert, I beat a hasty retreat for the safety of *Dove*.

Back at the boat, Winston and George were talking with three boatloads of happy, smiling Eskimo men and women who had been gathering murre eggs at Cape Lisburne. A huge wicker basket contained well over a hundred eggs. These unusual, multi-colored, speckled eggs were larger than a chicken's and rather pointed, enabling the egg to spin on a narrow rocky ledge rather than roll off easily.

> *Eighty different species of birds bring grace and song to the Arctic, sometimes all of them in one location. The most abundant seabird in the Arctic is the thick-billed murre or apka. They are superficially like penguins, both in their coloring and because they walk upright. The murre's wings are very short and narrow and they obtain most of their food by actually flying underwater.*
> **The Unbelievable Land—Birds in the Arctic, L.M. Tuck**

The chart showed an abandoned D.E.W. (distant early warning) line station at Cape Lisburne, which the Eskimos confirmed. They also said the cape area was mostly free of ice and would not be a problem to reach. The next day, under a windless, clear blue sky, *Dove* motored out of Marryatt Inlet toward Cape Lisburne.

Travelling from Marryatt Inlet through a perpetual maze of broken bergs and large ice floes was, as usual, a little unnerving, particularly when *Dove* was far offshore and leads—openings in the ice large enough to allow a vessel to pass through—became scarce. We took turns climbing the ratlines to scan the horizon for leads to take us back closer to shore. Eventually, after quite a struggle with the ice, we were rewarded with a close-up of the high, craggy cliffs of Cape Lisburne.

CAPE LISBURNE

The cape rises like a monolith out of the icy waters of the Chukchi Sea to an elevation of approximately 500 meters. The steep, slate-colored, jagged cliffs of the cape looked as if they had been struck by a monstrous tsunami (tidal wave) at some time that had shattered the face of the cliff. The narrow ledges and caves were home to innumerable seabirds, predominately murres and puffins. They dove and swam all about us, their raucous calls clearly audible above the roar of the engine and the occasional crash of bergs that split in the summer sun.

As *Dove* approached the abandoned D.E.W. station, a series of blinking lights, structures that looked like large fuel tanks, and a number of buildings came into view. As it turned out, the blinking lights marked an airstrip, the tanks were filled with fuel and water, and the buildings housed people and equipment. Cape Lisburne was anything but abandoned.

After the Second World War, 150 servicemen had been stationed here; now only 12 were needed. The eleven men and one woman, the cook, were under contract to maintain the airstrip and monitor the parabolic radar tower located atop the cape. During the winter, the 12-man crew is cut to four. You would have to enjoy isolation to work at this lonely installation.

The next morning, camera gear in hand, we rowed ashore with the intention of walking to the end of the runway to explore an old Eskimo ruin and the grave site of the first missionary to arrive in this area. As we strolled leisurely along the runway, George noticed a large grizzly bear snooping about one of the smaller outbuildings. When the bear began to ramble in our direction, we headed for the safety of the main building. We knew polar bears were common in this area, but grizzlies? Who would have thought?

The overseer of Cape Lisburne, a young man named Scott Pillars, who hails from Reed City, Michigan, at first seemed apprehensive and cool toward our arrival. However, after receiving the okay from his supervisor to allow us on the base, he was a gracious host, permitting us to use the showers, wash our clothes, and share some tasty meals with him and his men.

During the afternoon, the ice began steadily moving closer to shore. To escape this assault, a worried Winston decided to run *Dove* aground on the gravel beach near the mouth of a small stream. As soon as she was edged ashore, we secured the anchor to the stream bank.

The location proved ideal as the stream's current was strong enough to keep the ice away. What we needed now was a strong offshore wind to blow the ice far out to sea so we could be on our way.

The next day, Scott took us to the top of Cape Lisburne to photograph the parabolic facility and surrounding area. From the sea, the silver-domed structure, set high above and

between several slender rock pinnacles, looked like an illustration from a sci-fi fantasy. The view from atop the cape was spectacular; we could see for miles. However, the wind was staggering. I literally had to crawl to the edge of the cliff and lie on my back with my feet dug in to photograph the base far below. *Dove* looked like a tiny toy boat tied to the

miniature estuary. As I scanned the eastern horizon, the ice seemed to go on forever like a gigantic slab of white marble, a swath of brilliant blue water separating it from the bronzed land.

First mate, George Hone

Since the strong winds at the summit were funneled down through the valley and fired directly at *Dove*, we were forced to leave the friendly hospitality of Cape Lisburne on Sunday, July 1, at 2400 hours, in search of a safer anchorage. Winston figured that anchoring in the mouth of the Thetis River, about 19 km away, would be a safe haven. Wrong—the Thetis River almost proved to be our journey's end.

With only two hours sleep under my belt, I was almost asleep standing up at the helm when my shift ended at four in the morning. No sooner had I fallen asleep than I was abruptly awakened by Winston yelling, "Wake up, Lenny, and give George a hand with the anchor."

Rubbing the sleep from my eyes, I groggily but hastily emerged from the cozy cabin into a dark, angry, and howling 40-knot wind. The expression on Winston's face told me we were in serious trouble. As I made my way toward the bow, George threw the anchor overboard. He yelled to me, "Keep an eye on the dinghy!"

I had just grabbed hold of the dinghy when a violent gust of wind almost tore it from my hands and blew it over the side. As I fought to keep the dinghy under control, Winston hollered over the wind, "Make sure you set the anchor real good, George."

He had, and it was a good thing, too. The anchor held, but the fierceness of the wind heeled *Dove* over at a very precarious angle and knocked her broadside against a sandbar. If Winston and George weren't scared to death, I know I was. Winston bellowed again, "George, get the anchor up. We gotta get outta here!"

George was happy to oblige. The throbbing veins of his neck stood out, as did the muscles and sinews of his arms, as he slowly but surely, one link at a time, began dragging the anchor aboard. He cursed into the wind, "Winston—what the hell are you doing!" as Winston steered *Dove* over the top of the anchor. Next he yelled to me, "Lenny, keep pointing at the anchor so Winston will know where it is!"

It was nearly impossible to point toward the anchor with one hand and keep the dinghy from going airborne with the other, but somehow I managed. Struggling with a strength I never saw in him before, George hauled the anchor aboard while Winston navigated *Dove* away from the sandbar under full power. Shortly afterwards, *Dove* left the shallow Thetis River and nosed her way into the wind-whipped and wild Chukchi Sea. About eight hours later, the wind died and we were once again stopped by the ice. We dropped the anchor into the mud just a little northeast of Cape Beaufort. After discussing our near-tragedy over a bite to eat and feeling ready for some well-earned "R 'n' R," Winston and I rowed ashore, 30-30 in hand. With the danger of polar bears on the ice and grizzlies on the land, we weren't taking any chances.

Stepping ashore, Winston and I were immediately attacked by a multitude of implaca-ble mosquitoes.

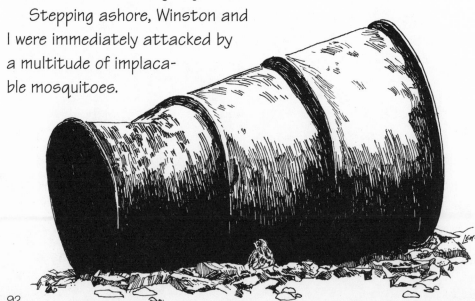

Each step we took brought forth dark clouds of buzzing rein-
forcements. The mosquitoes were so dense that our clothes
took on a fur-like appearance. Before leaving the boat we had
applied mosquito repellent to the uncovered parts of our
bodies and, although I occasionally had to wipe them from
behind my glasses and spit them out of my mouth, I was never
once bitten.

A large dark object, prominent against the cloudless eastern sky, aroused our curiosity. At sea, people are often fooled
by the appearance of objects lying on the horizon because they
appear larger and nearer than they actually are. What seemed
at first a short jaunt proved otherwise. An hour later, the
object still appeared the same size, except that now we could
see two of them.

As we finally drew near, the mystery was solved. The objects
were a giant drilling rig on treads with a utility trailer attached;
these rigs are used for taking soil samples in the search for oil.
At first we though the rig was abandoned. However, with the
discovery of a large cache of 200-liter fuel drums nearby, and
summer just around the corner, we figured the mechanical behemoth would soon be operational. Since Dove's fuel tanks were a
bit on the low side, we hoped the drums contained diesel, but no
such luck. They were filled with unleaded gasoline.

Being fully clothed, the long walk under the hot sun made us
thirsty. Searching the many compartments of both vehicles, we
jokingly said, "Wouldn't it be great if we found a dozen cold
beers?" Just as we were about to give up, Winston found two
tins of cool pop under the drilling rig's seat. What a bonus!

While we relaxed, drinking our pop in the shade of the drilling
rig, a small silver-colored fox stepped suddenly from the lumpy

tundra close to a nearby pond and began to bark at us. I thought this was unusual behavior until it dawned on me that the fox probably had a den full of kits nearby and was trying to coax us away.

We decided to walk a little farther to check out the ice conditions which had halted our progress. The fox, darting in and out of the tundra along the bank, followed until we came to

a deep, slow-moving stream. Since we couldn't cross the stream, we headed back to the boat. The little fox kept us company as far as the drilling rig, then headed back toward the pond and disappeared.

Monday, July 3

Departed 0630; by 0900 the leads had all closed until we had no choice but to tie onto a large berg grounded in about 1.5 meters of water. Travelled only 7.5 km; looks like we could be here awhile. Winston and I trudged along the beach to check out a large pressure ridge of ice yet to break away from the shore, and I found a small, green Japanese glass float which I kept for a souvenir.

Winston securing ice hook

Tuesday, July 4

Drifted and motored about 5 km today. *Dove* ran aground near the first entrance to Kasegaluk Lagoon. George rowed the anchor out to deeper water which enabled us to winch *Dove* off the sandy shoal. We are now hooked to another ice floe.

Adrift—almost the story of my life. At times I've had direction, I'm not sure how meaningful, but at least there seemed to be a Point A and a Point B, with a more-or-less straight line connecting the two. But at this point in time, I am without a real direction; like *Dove* through the ice, I travel the course of least resistance.

Kukpowruk Pass, the first of many entrances leading into Kasegaluk Lagoon, was just a hop, skip and jump away. However, we needed a little blue water to get us there. We had just snuggled into our sleeping bags for a good night's sleep when suddenly *Dove* was struck by a little gust of wind like a divine call of Providence, because when Winston got up to investigate, a small lead had opened up, enough for *Dove* to sneak into the ice-free lagoon. Like an army pursuing a defeated foe, the ice followed us through the gap. After anchoring and re-anchoring several times, we finally escaped the relentless approach of the ice about 2 km inside the entrance.

The following morning, I looked through the tinted plexiglass window of the cozy, wheelhouse at a desolate hut on a narrow stretch of flat land that seemed to disappear into eternity. I could visualize an Eskimo hunter dragging his kill onto the beach, his wife waiting with a sharp-honed oolu (knife) to skillfully gut and skin the beast. However, in days of old, the run-down wooden shack wouldn't have been there; a skin tent would have stood in its place. I couldn't imagine living in a tent under such extreme cold and wind conditions, especially since I hail from a much warmer climate and grew up with central heating.

In the afternoon, Winston and I went ashore to investigate the derelict shack and the ice conditions on the other side of the narrow peninsula. We were astonished by the damage caused by the 20- to 30-knot winds during the night. As far as we could see along the shore, there was ice, some chunks as thick as 2 meters, some stacked one atop the other. The entire Chukchi Sea looked like a gigantic winter graveyard covered by tombstones of ice—not a drop of water could be seen. To think that *Dove* might have been caught in that chaotic and hazardous jumble of ice was unfathomable. I doubt she would have survived such an ordeal. I thanked God for the little puff of wind which had awakened Winston the previous night, and the 300-meter-wide stretch of lowland separating us from the onslaught of the ice.

Thursday, July 6

Trying to understand the ways of the ice is like trying to understand a woman. Just when I think I've got it all figured out, logic takes a major twist. I'm learning that women and ice have at least one thing in common—both should be treated with respect.

Friday, July 7

Departed Kasegaluk Lagoon 0930. Made another 9 km before being forced by the ice to retreat through Akunik Pass. At 1300, we dropped the hook once again in Kasegaluk Lagoon. Still 92 km to Point Barrow; at this rate, it will take ten more days.

Saturday, July 8

Exactly two months have passed since our tearful departure from home.

We had it easy today; not too much ice. Yes, it was very relaxing until we reached the ice guarding Akoliakatat Pass that leads into the seemingly-endless Kasegaluk Lagoon. It's one pass I'll not soon forget, as our journey almost came to an end.

Being caught in the center of a swirling eddy of ice was not my idea of fun—especially when all the leads were slamming shut. One last lead remained open and, as I watched from my position at the top of the ratlines, a sweating Winston throttled *Dove* full speed ahead toward our avenue of escape. I felt like a jockey riding a spirited thoroughbred toward the finish wire; except that now, instead of another race horse, a huge block of ice was closing fast on the outside and, unfortunately, won by a nose. However, *Dove's* momentum drove her up onto the ice floe where she slid along on her side. I quickly scrambled down from my precarious position. Since I was hanging way out over the ice, I figured that, if I was going to fall into the icy water, it might as well be from the deck—not as far to fall. Luckily, *Dove* splashed unscathed into the icy water on the other side of the ice floe and managed to beat and bash her way toward an open lead. Finally, after about a half-hour of winding and twisting through the ice-choked current flowing out of Akoliakatat Pass,

Dove again slipped into the safety of Kasegaluk Lagoon.

When *Dove* was securely and safely anchored on the far side of the lagoon, I watched the mad jumble of ice floes still trying to squeeze through the narrow pass, and wrote:

July 8

I wonder how many more of these heart-stopping episodes we will have to survive before we get out of this never-ending maze of ice once and for all. I fear the worst is yet to come, because it seems that the further north we travel, the more difficult the ice conditions become.

The next morning, under beautiful sunny skies, *Dove* approached the small town of Wainwright. Under normal conditions, the 12-hour trip would have taken six; ice has a way of slowing things down.

When we were less than 1.5 km from the entrance to Wainwright, Winston decided to run *Dove* ashore to escape the slowly churning ice floes that seemed intent on imprisoning us. Some Eskimos who were hunting nearby in the midst of the ice gave us directions on how to reach a large expanse of water leading into Wainwright. Two Eskimos in a small aluminum skiff found us surrounded by ice and offered to lead us out. But their boat was lightweight and drew only centimeters compared with *Dove*, so we were unable to follow them. They were amazing, a delight to watch. At times they stood on the ice, then lifted their boat and slid it across the ice to the open water on the other side.

We expected to spend the night on the beach, but after

hours of waiting, a skinny lead finally opened. Dove dashed for the opening, racing a large ice floe that was steadily closing in to block our route of escape. Dove managed to squeeze through, leaving the way to Wainwright virtually ice-free. We all breathed a sigh of relief and agreed when George exclaimed, "We deserve double rums tonight!"

WAINWRIGHT

Originally known as "the place where storms are not very bad," Wainwright was more progressive than other villages we had visited. The houses were, for the most part, in excellent shape and an atmosphere of well-being seemed to permeate the community. This was because of the current employment boom due to the building of a pipeline to Southern California, or so we were told by a couple of Eskimo boys. However, they weren't sure if the pipes would be carrying oil or water. Judging by the huge amount of insulation around the pipes, I guessed that water was the intended commodity.

One thing Wainwright had in common with other communities was that the kids seemed to take delight in breaking windows and having rock fights. As we approached some boys engaged in a rock fight, a couple of them sneaked off behind a building. When they emerged, they were surprised to find me looking them square in the eye. Obviously, they had planned on beaning us from behind. I kept a wary eye on them until we were well out of range.

A few nights earlier, I experienced a rather erotic dream. I awoke at the dream's conclusion and translated it into poetry. At first, I called it "The Dream," but "San" seemed more appropriate, as she often ignites inspiration within me.

"San"

As the sleeping sailor of the sea
dreamt of home, wife and family,
a mysterious maiden of the night
came calling in the misty moonlight;
her face angelic, her smile divine,
and her body much too beautiful to define
was dressed in a gown of gossamer silk
as rich and smooth as creamy milk.

Within the tiny confines of the yacht
he tossed and turned upon the cot;
blinking his eyes and shaking his head
wondering if he were alive or dead!
But as she drew near with open arms
dropping her gown, exposing her charms,
she spoke in a voice so soft and sweet,
"It's time, my sailor, for us to meet."

Kneeling down, she took his hand
saying, "Please, I hope you'll understand;
like you, I'm as lonely as can be,
adrift on the wind and endless sea
of lapping waves and frothing foam,
a long, long way from home,
from the one I love with all my heart
wishing the while we weren't apart."

Her words, they lulled him like a song
as a voice within said, "Be strong!"
But as she pouted purple-stainéd lips,
swaying to and fro from her hips,
whether for pleasure or for whim
she slowly winked her eye at him;
and as she placed his hand upon her breast,
he gasped, "No! Please, you must get dressed!"

"Don't worry, sailor, it's not as it seems;
for alas, I'm just a part of your dreams.
So please, let me love you like I used to,
for you need me as I need you.
Can't you see, I'm the one you left at home,
across the vast seas you daringly roam;
so quickly, dearest, before you awake,
reach out and your desires I will slake!"

As he reached for her within the night,
she began to fade into the light.
"Please wait!" he said, "I must know your name,
if this is real or some sort of game?"
As she quietly slid through his finger tips,
he could see words forming on her lips,
"My name is Sandra, but you call me San;
I am your woman and you, you are my man."

A strong wind had been blowing for some time; we hoped it
would blow the ice far out to sea enabling us to reach our next
destination, Barrow, Alaska. We knew that the ice had yet to

open up because the Barrow radio station, KBRW, reported: "People should stay off the beach as polar bears have been seen prowling there on the ice."

While we relaxed and listened to the radio, Winston happened to glance out the porthole and noticed that *Dove* was getting dangerously close to shore. He calculated that because the wind had shifted during the night, the anchor chain must have wrapped around the anchor, causing it to break free. We were fortunate to be awake or *Dove* could easily have drifted up against the muddy banks of the Kuk River inlet.

Tuesday, July 11

Departed Wainwright at 0600. It's a beautiful day; the sun is shining brightly and there's not a cloud in the sky; more importantly—no ice!

Late in the day, as *Dove* motored by Peard Bay, an archeologist who was working at an old, abandoned whaling site hailed us on the VHF radio. She told us that she could scarcely believe her eyes when she looked up from her work and spotted a vessel— especially a small sailboat—so early in the year. She was talkative and inquisitive, asking many questions about our journey, as well as telling us about some of her archeological discoveries. Shortly after that, we received another communication from a woman pilot who had just left Barrow. She reported that the route was pretty much clear of ice—the kind of news we enjoyed hearing.

Not far ahead, the chart showed a monument commemorating the famous American humorist, Will Rogers, and his pilot friend, Wiley Post who had died in a plane crash August 15,

1935, at a place close to the spot shown on the chart. However, just before reaching the monument, a heavy fog drifted in and cut our visibility to a minimum. Although we could vaguely make out what looked like a statue on the shore, we had to pass it by. The closer we got to Barrow, the denser the fog became, until all three of us were forced to be on deck, straining our eyes to avoid hitting large chunks of ice which floated intermittently into view then seemed to vanish into thin air.

After hours of making our way through fog and ice, Barrow finally came into view, but the main body of ice had closed to within about 30 meters of the low sandy beach, Winston opted to anchor Dove in Elson Lagoon, nine kilometers east of Barrow. Unfortunately, the lagoon was frozen solid so we had no choice but to return to Barrow. On Wednesday, July 12, 0600, we warily dropped the hook between Barrow and the ice—ice that at any time could trap us and push Dove onto the beach.

Barrow to Herschel Island

BARROW

Barrow, the northernmost town in the United States, is located 190 kilometers above the Arctic Circle, where the Chukchi and Beaufort seas blend together. At first glimpse, Barrow appears to be an up-to-date town with all the modern conveniences. However, when observed more closely, you can see, intermingled among the contemporary apartments, houses and business establishments, dwellings that house the original inhabitants of Barrow—the Inupiats, the "real" or "genuine people."

The homes of the Inupiats look much the same as the white man's, except that they are usually surrounded by racks of drying meat, animal skins, and baleen from the bowhead whale. Besides the usual hodgepodge of skidoos [motorized vehicles with a set of skis in front and treads at the rear] in every state of repair imaginable, skinboat frames, a variety of sleds, and other equipment were cast in disarray about the yards, along with large and not too friendly Huskies. On more than one

occasion, I found myself hastily vacating the vicinity of someone's yard, a growling Husky at my heels.

So far, wherever we stopped, people had always been friendly; Barrow was no exception. Some people actually went out of their way to meet us and invite us into their homes; two such people were Kenji Yoshikawa and Parker Rittgers.

Shortly after our arrival, I was standing on the beach waiting for George and Winston to row ashore, when I was approached by what looked like an Inupiat riding a four-wheeled ATV. However, after shaking hands with the wide-smiling stranger, I discovered that he was none other than Kenji, the Japanese sailor we had heard about in Nome whose sailboat was trapped in the ice many kilometers offshore. He was surprised to learn we had heard about him and his adventures aboard *Hoki Mae* (Return). We were equally surprised to learn that his boat, rather than being trapped in the middle of the Chukchi Sea, was frozen in the ice at Elson Lagoon. The only problem was that it was on a

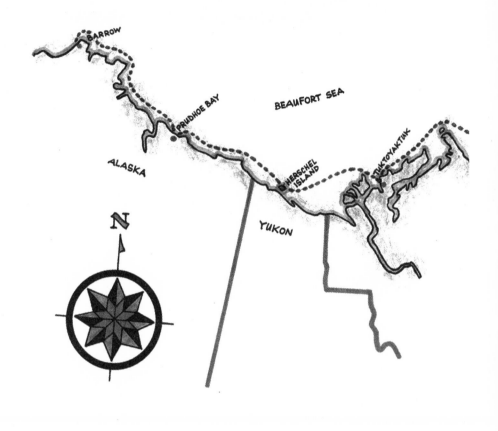

bit of an uphill slant due to a shift in the ice. (Later, we learned that *Hoki Mae* was unscathed once the ice had melted and released the boat from its clutches.)

Kenji invited us to the apartment where he was temporarily living with his American-Chinese girlfriend. While we took turns enjoying hot showers, Kenji prepared a delicious, tangy Mexican taco dinner, topped off with strawberry yogurt. He also introduced us to maktak (bowhead whale blubber); with dark, slate-colored skin and pinkish flesh, it looked much like a slice of watermelon. The skin, about 2 cm thick, was quite chewy; the texture and flavor of the maktak was much like sashimi. Although George and Winston didn't find it palatable, I found it quite appetizing and enjoyed several pieces.

At first we thought Kenji was attempting to traverse the Northwest Passage, but we learned that he was a scientist investigating whether methane gas, escaping from the permafrost, was having any effect on the ozone layer. Although Kenji planned to remain at Barrow for another year, he was already in the midst of organizing yet another scientific expedition. This energetic, adventurous man, who at one time had walked across the Sahara Desert, was negotiating with the Russians to explore and study a small island in the Arctic Ocean where traces of prehistoric saber-toothed tigers have been found.

During the evening, while we were refill-ing our empty diesel

Inupiat kids

containers at the local gas station, the congenial Parker Rittgers introduced himself and invited us to have supper at his house the following day. His wife, Kit, and her friend, Diane, served up another delicious taco dinner, complete with ice cream. The friendly and devout hospitality and atmosphere reminded me of our earlier dinner with the Jacobson family at False Pass.

Just as we were about to leave, Parker showed us a beautiful, laminated hardwood harp he had built for his wife. Since the harp, with its soothing, melodious sounds, is one of my favorite instruments, I asked Kit if she would be kind enough to play something for us. I could see the pleasure in her eyes as she smilingly accepted, saying, "I'll probably be too self-conscious." If she was nervous, I doubt that anyone noticed when the delightful music filled the room.

While wandering about Barrow exploring the

sights, I met several Inupiat children playing on the beach. They seemed happy and inquisitive, anxious to pose for my camera, except for one pretty girl. She was adamant about not having her photo taken. She even refused to open her eyes, and eventually she stood up, pulling her coat over her head.

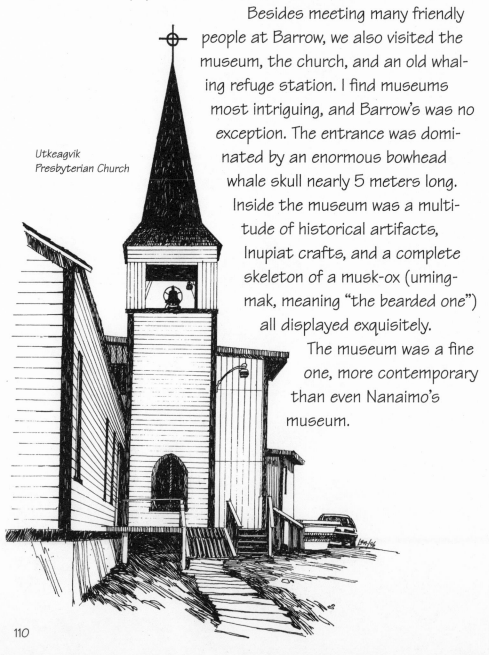

Utkeagvik
Presbyterian Church

Besides meeting many friendly people at Barrow, we also visited the museum, the church, and an old whaling refuge station. I find museums most intriguing, and Barrow's was no exception. The entrance was dominated by an enormous bowhead whale skull nearly 5 meters long. Inside the museum was a multitude of historical artifacts, Inupiat crafts, and a complete skeleton of a musk-ox (umingmak, meaning "the bearded one") all displayed exquisitely.

The museum was a fine one, more contemporary than even Nanaimo's museum.

The entrance to the Utkeagvik Presbyterian Church, built in 1949 but established in 1889, wasn't as dramatic as the museum's, but the stained glass panels depicting passages and scenes from the Bible were a sight to behold. The church seemed like a beautiful place for prayer and the singing of hymns.

Another significant building, the former Point Barrow Refuge Station, built in 1889 by Charles Brower, was erected to provide aid for stranded whalers.

The station is operational today, except now it's called Brower's Cafe. On the beach directly in front of the cafe stands an impressive arch made from the jawbones of a bowhead whale, approximately six meters in length. As we posed for a photo beneath the jawbones, it was easy to visualize how a whale had swallowed Jonah.

Since the main body of ice around Barrow never really melts, but disintegrates slowly with the changing of the winds throughout the summer, it is not considered a very safe anchorage. Earlier, we had witnessed the wrath and aftermath of a violent storm, the ice stacked high along the shore. Needless to say, we were more than a little concerned and nervous about *Dove's* position and anxious to be on our way.

Wednesday, July 12

Departed Barrow 2300. We didn't get far before the ice stopped us cold. However, Elson Lagoon, now unbelievably devoid of ice, offered safe refuge. The ice pack, still intent on stopping our progress to Prudhoe Bay, stubbornly followed us into the lagoon, forcing us to move our anchorage several times.

Friday, July 14

Severe ice conditions outside the lagoon forced us to retreat once again. We had to anchor *Dove* several times before finally escaping the relentless bergs which followed us wherever we moved. Winston somehow pulled a muscle, "from the root of my balls to my groin." He seems to be in quite a bit of pain; sure hope he'll be all right.

Saturday, July 15

Caught in the doldrums of the arctic ice, *Dove* rests peacefully at anchor in Elson Lagoon. The sky, cloudy and filled with rain, presses down on the submissive land. The ice waits like a siege of soldiers just beyond the natural border of Sanigaruak Island. The tide will soon change and like yesterday, an army of stampeding bergs will once again burst through the narrow gap of Sanigaruak Pass in hope of capturing the beleaguered *Dove*. So until the inevitable occurs, I shall continue to describe the events of this voyage and my thoughts onto the damp pages of this journal.

At this moment, a warm fire is chuckling in the small airtight woodstove. The trill of someone playing a piano on the Barrow radio station can be heard, as well as the occasional soft-toned voice of an Inupiat hunter talking on the VHF. A tired and aching Winston lounges on his bunk reading a Louis L'Amour western, while an invariably hungry George relaxes as well. We would rather be chugging through the ice, knocking off kilometers, but we have learned that it is better to be patient than to buck the idiosyncrasies of Mother Nature.

A few rays of sunshine have escaped the imprisonment of the clouds; I can see them shimmering on the wavelets. Do your stuff, sun—melt the ice!!

Dinners aboard *Dove III* were hardly gourmet, but for the most part palatable. Three of the most popular dishes were Dove Goolash, Smashed Eggs and Ham, and Portly Kentucky-fried Pancakes.

George's favorite, which he aptly named "Dove Goolash," takes 2-1/2 cups of pert, polished minute rice boiled to perfection in 5 cups of chemically-flavored water. Add 1 can of tepid, pallid peas; stir well. Next, what is goulash without a large can of muddled meatballs conglobulated in a grey, glutinous gravy? Dove Goolash is best served in a pail, slathered with globs of blood-red ketchup. Feeds three snow-blind sailors. *Bon appetit!*

Lenny's "Smashed Eggs and Ham" is best prepared during a 35-knot gale. First, gently crush 6 eggs, shells and all, into a greasy, preheated frying pan; deftly flipped, the mixture produces 6-1/2 smashed eggs. Thickly slice 1 can of gelatinous ham, char slightly and serve with the eggs over blackened toast and tease with a splattering of tantalizing tomato ketchup. This recipe is a sure-fire hit for three starving seamen who haven't eaten in as many weeks.

Chef Winston's specialty was "Portly Kentucky-fried Pancakes." To feed three unsuspecting sailors, use 4 cups of instant pancake mix and add chemically-flavored water (quite possibly the main ingredient); stir until mixture is the consistency of thick, lumpy wallpaper paste. Spoon ingredients into preheated, overly-greased pan and fry until crispy on the outside and gooey in the middle. Lather with margarine and slurpy syrup; serve on plate or lap (depending on sea conditions). A platter of Portly Kentucky-fried Pancakes is guaranteed to be a sticky, finger-lickin' favorite.

The ice barrier on the other side of Sanigaruak Island finally drifted off. On July 16, at 1145 hours, we were able to break for the open sea. However, two-thirds of the way through the Plover Islands, we were again besieged by the ice. After struggling for almost two hours, close to shore and under almost full power,

Dove struck a well-camouflaged, semi-submerged ice floe. Up to this point, *Dove* had bashed her way through many identical leads with little or no trouble. But because the bottom of the sea had been stirred up by a previous storm, what appeared to be a lead between two ice floes was, in fact, one very large berg. The piece of ice joining the two bergs was covered in sand and mud just below the surface and was impossible to see.

Dove had rammed many bergs before with very little problem. She usually bulldozed her way up onto the ice which would either break apart or push her back into the water. But not this time. *Dove* came to a sudden and violent halt. Swaying precariously in the ratlines, I watched with dismay as George, who was standing near the bow, went sprawling face down on the steel deck. I immediately looked back over my shoulder to see how Winston had fared, but he was nowhere to be seen. I could hear him moaning in the cockpit, however, and yelled to George, "You'd better check on Winston. I think he's hurt."

We were lucky—very lucky. I shudder to think what might have occurred if I hadn't been hanging on so tight, or if the mast had let go and thundered to the deck, or if *Dove* had been holed. Somewhat shaken, I climbed down to the cockpit where Winston sat huddled, a worried George standing over him. One hand covered his mouth while the other held a badly smashed and bloody denture plate. Although his upper gums were severely lacerated, none of his bottom teeth appeared damaged. Fortunately, he had brought along a spare plate, and even though he was still in pain, it wasn't long before he was his old smiling self once again.

Not long after *Dove*'s brutal impact with the berg, the main body of pack ice began to close in under cover of heavy fog and cold drizzling rain. As *Dove* wove her way through the intricate maze of ice, Winston pointed and asked, "Didn't we pass that chunk of ice before?"

It was hard to determine if we were running in circles. After meandering through the icy labyrinth for a long time, getting farther and farther from shore, Winston decided to tie *Dove* to an ice floe for a while. After a short time, we heard what sounded like rifle shots in the distance. We followed the sounds through the jumbled ice until we found several Inupiat men and one woman hunting seals. Judging by the expressions on their faces, they were shocked to see a sailboat appear suddenly out of the fog. We asked directions, and the woman pointed toward a lead which ultimately led us out of the ice-clogged Beaufort Sea to Point Drew.

July 16, 2441 hours

We are anchored off Point Drew in Smith Bay and have been pushing off bergs constantly for the past hour and a half. Winston and George are now in bed and asleep, hopefully. Since the bay looks relatively clear of ice, I'll try to get a little shut-eye—0600 comes early. It's been a long 25-kilometer day.

Having daylight for a full 24 hours takes a bit of adjustment, especially when a person is accustomed to darkness at night. Since our shifts consisted of two hours on and four off, the light didn't have much effect on our sleep patterns while travelling. Getting to sleep was a problem at times, but I found that reading a good pocket novel or listening to some tunes on the tape deck was as good as a sleeping pill. It wasn't until we visited a village or town that I felt odd. Because it is as bright at midnight as it is at noon, I expected more activity and the stores to be open no matter what time the clock said.

Monday, July 17
Departed Point Drew 0830. Cloudy and drizzly, but hardly any ice!

At 1145, *Dove* came abeam another D.E.W. parabolic installation at Pitt Point, otherwise known as "Lonely." I remembered hearing a native's voice on the VHF saying mournfully, "I'm down at Lonely. I can't get home, too much ice. Tell my wife I won't be home tonight." My guess is that Lonely got its name from just such a message.

Our progress from Point Drew to Prudhoe Bay was, thankfully, mostly uneventful; at least, it was accident-free. Although the 24-hour sun was not visible due to thick cloud cover, the weather was much warmer and the sea essentially free of ice. Near evening, however, an influx of pack ice and heavy, thick fog forced *Dove* to slow down and eventually come to a standstill. Comfortably secured to an ice floe, we enjoyed a bowl of hot tomato-rice soup before we finally broke through the ice, arriving at Prudhoe Bay at ten o'clock, Tuesday morning, July 18.

PRUDHOE BAY
Prudhoe Bay wasn't at all what I had imagined. I never antici-pated a red-carpet welcome, and had mentioned fixing some mush (porridge) for breakfast, to which Winston had replied, "I expect they'll feed us bacon and eggs." What a joke! Bacon and eggs? Ha! We weren't even allowed ashore.

July 18

George and Winston claimed that the town was
inhabited by 20,000 people; perhaps at one time,
but not anymore. Only a fraction of the population
remained; I expect most worked for the conglomer-
ate of large American oil companies that seemed to
own and control the whole of Prudhoe Bay. This
place is the worst example of a company monopoliz-
ing a town that I've ever experienced. If a conglomer-
ate does indeed govern Prudhoe Bay, it is strictly a
dictatorship. Not only are we not allowed to go
ashore, we are not allowed to visit the Inupiat
village, Dead Horse, located about 5 kilometers
further into the bay. We have been told to leave.

Although going ashore was strictly prohibited, we were eventually allowed to anchor in the bay overnight. From what I could
see from the boat, Prudhoe Bay was a hive of activity; trucks
and machines of every description were constantly on the move.
It was fun to watch the activity along the shore, relax in the
sun and catch up on some sleep.

If there is anything positive to report about our treatment in
Prudhoe Bay, I should mention the skipper aboard Barge 213. He
seemed genuinely upset and apologized for the way we had been
treated. Before we left, he donated 65 liters of diesel and a number
of detailed American navigational charts that we didn't have.

Wednesday, July 19

Departed Prudhoe Bay 1330; raw and cloudy with
an occasional heavy mist. The weather forecast
calls for strong winds and 1.5 meter seas.
Hopefully, no ice.

Thursday, July 20

Took turns at the helm, two hours on, four off. Cloudy with a heavy mist and occasional rain. Not much ice to speak of; no wind either.

Friday, July 21

The strong winds and steep seas caught up to us about 4.5 km away from Herschel Island, Yukon, 0400.

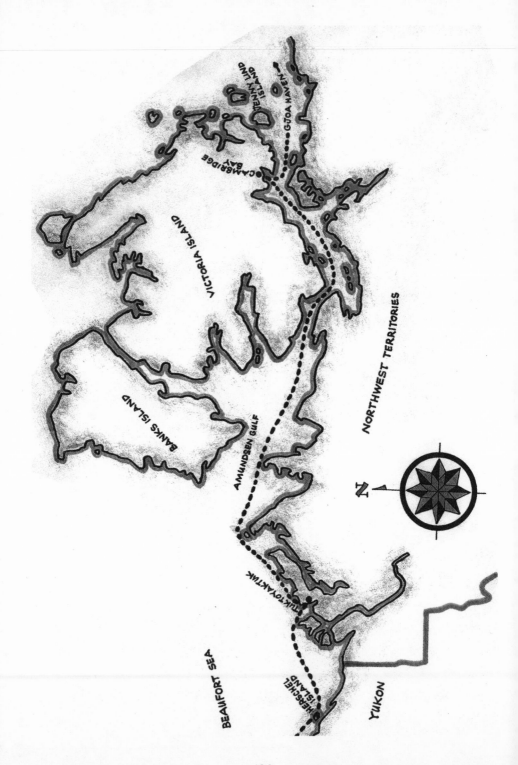

The Yukon to Gjoa Haven

HERSCHEL ISLAND

It was early on a dismal morning when *Dove* motored past the old whaling station built on a very narrow peninsula, barely above sea level, known as Herschel Island. Up ahead, a Canadian Coast Guard vessel lay at anchor in Ptarmigan Bay just off Simpson Point (Kuvuraq); from a distance, it looked rather small, even fragile. However, once we rafted alongside *Ivik*, we could see she was a stout, powerful vessel of considerable size; in comparison, *Dove* was a dwarf.

The crew were friendly and inquisitive, asking many questions about our voyage. The skipper, who was asleep at the time, later gave us 90 liters of diesel which ensured us reaching our next destination, Tuktoyaktuk. In addition, he gave us an ice report which showed an ice-free journey to Tuktoyaktuk and beyond; Cambridge Bay, however, was still icebound.

We were anxious to explore the old buildings of the once-busy whaling station and R.C.M.P. post, but after dropping the hook in tiny, shallow Pauline Cove (Ilutaq), we opted for bed instead. We were just too tired. About four hours later, I was awakened by the clamor of a small single-engine amphibious plane taxiing past *Dove*. I watched as it disgorged three tourists and the pilot onto a small

floating dock. I later learned that their short excursion from Inuvik cost $900, and I remember feeling a little angry. After all, they had simply flown in, whereas we had had to work hard to arrive at the same destination.

After brunch, we rowed ashore to investigate the once-flourishing town. The well-preserved main building, now a museum, had at one time been the Pacific Steam Whaling community house (1893) and, later, the R.C.M.P. detachment headquarters and barracks (1903). The multi-layered, painted door, deeply etched by weather, opened into a long, narrow hallway leading to several large and spacious rooms. One well-lit room accommodated some glass showcases displaying many interesting old whaling and Inuit artifacts. There was an old-fashioned kitchen complete with

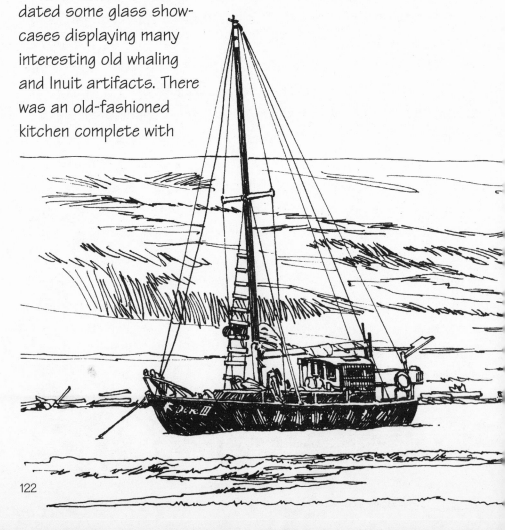

pantry. The room we enjoyed the most was furnished with a large wooden table resembling a picnic table, a bench on each side, and a bookshelf holding three thick photo albums showing life on the island from the early whaling days to the present.

Several other buildings, such as the Northern Whaling and Trading Company store (1926), Northern Whaling and Trading Company customs bonded warehouse (1926), and the Pacific Steam Whaling Company blubber house (1890s) safeguarded memorabilia of long-vanished whaling vessels; bones of every description and size could also be seen. It seemed a privilege, an honor, to walk the heavy-planked wooden floors, my footsteps echoing where mounties, whalers and parka-clad Inuits once trod.

The museum and other buildings, open only six months of the year, are maintained by Inuit park rangers. Other residents included an Inuit family that lives in a small cabin— the only building open year-round—while other Inuits were spending the summer in a log cabin built in 1968.

Deborah Robinson was visiting the log cabin residents. She had moved to Inuvik, N.W.T., five years earlier to escape what she called "the sick society of Vancouver." She visited us aboard *Dove* the night before we left Herschel Island. As she sat drinking her hot chocolate, she asked, "What sort of men are you to undertake such a dangerous trip?"

Winston replied for the three of us, "We're just ordinary guys who thought it would be a great sailing adventure."

Deborah was a character, with a laid-back manner, and I could see that she would fit in well with the people and environment of the high north.

The wind howled steadily across the low peninsula and brought intermittent barrages of heavy mist and rain. Despite the weather, I hiked across the wet, spongy tundra, determined to photograph and film some graves high atop a hill, surprisingly green in a landscape of grey and brown, that overlooked the

contemporary log cabin

lonely outpost of Herschel Island. Along the way, I passed about a dozen old whaler graves, conspicuously marked by large, white-washed wooden slabs and crosses. Near the base of the hill stood a mound of earth, an Inuit ice hut used for storing meat and fish at a constant minus 14 degrees. The aging wood-slat-

1889 WHALING CREW

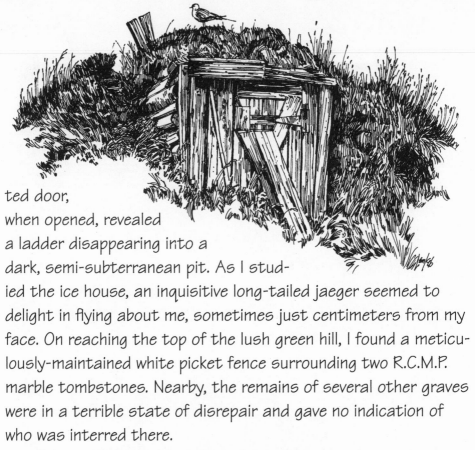

ted door,
when opened, revealed
a ladder disappearing into a
dark, semi-subterranean pit. As I stud-
ied the ice house, an inquisitive long-tailed jaeger seemed to
delight in flying about me, sometimes just centimeters from my
face. On reaching the top of the lush green hill, I found a meticu-
lously-maintained white picket fence surrounding two R.C.M.P.
marble tombstones. Nearby, the remains of several other graves
were in a terrible state of disrepair and gave no indication of
who was interred there.

While sitting atop the hill on the soft wet tundra, my back to
the wind, I noticed colorful explosions of flowers across the landscape; a favorite of mine was like a puff of cotton. In the
distance, I could see what looked like another graveyard. Anxious
to explore it, I headed downhill quickly. It was difficult wading
through the waist-deep leafy willows growing along the foot of
the hill, but I finally arrived at what was indeed an old Inuit grave
site. The names and dates on the weather-battered grave markers were illegible save one that read simply, "John." I was
saddened to see so many smaller graves that probably belonged
to children. The permafrost had been unkind to this particular
site; several coffins had been pushed to the surface, bursting

the seams of the aged wood. Whole skeletons and gaping skulls could be seen, putting me in touch with my own mortality.

Although the wind whistled about me in the old abandoned graveyard, I felt a sense of calmness in the air. Although words of endearment and tears of love had long since been swept away on the wind, the dilapidated, hand-hewn picket fences and grave markers stood as a testament that someone at some time had cared deeply for these people.

On my return to the boat, I was greeted by a smiling Winston carrying our towels. I could scarce believe my ears when he said we could have a sauna.

"A sauna!" I exclaimed, "Way

out here?" Thanks to a kind local, it wasn't long before the heat from a well-fed woodstone had sweat trickling down my lobster-red body; it was glorious. As the wind whipped and buffeted the small cedar shake building, I thought, it's good to be alive!

July 23

Departed Herschel Island 0715. While hoisting the anchor from the gluey, grey mud, the holding power was so intense that the anchor shaft bent. The day was windy, as usual, and right on the nose. Sea conditions were very uncomfortable.

As *Dove* motored toward Tuktoyaktuk, a message came over the VHF asking all mariners to keep an eye out for a 37-year-old Inuit man who had gone missing while paddling his grey and green kayak. My heart went out to him as I stood my shifts and scanned the ice-cold, white-capped green waters of the Beaufort Sea. Nowhere did we see a lost kayaker; I never saw so much as a floating log. Just outside of Tuktoyaktuk, we heard the good news—the lost kayaker had been found safe and sound. I was instantly flooded with a sense of relief; after all, being lost at sea was something that could happen to us.

TUKTOYAKTUK

The small hamlet of Tuktoyaktuk, "place where deer cross," was much the same as the other towns we had seen along the arctic coastline. Many of the small houses, built atop stilts, were erected from pre-packaged kits which arrived in large metal containers via Mackenzie River barges. The atmosphere was quieter than on the American side and we could walk the dirt roads three abreast without fear of being run over by a speeding ATV or pickup truck.

Since the "boom and bust" of the oil industry in the Tuktoyaktuk area, little was available in the way of employment or commerce. Retail shops, restaurants, bars or liquor stores were virtually non-existent, but it was possible to enjoy a coffee or meal at the Pingo Lodge, although pricey in comparison to my hometown of Nanaimo. Liquor of any kind was out of the question; all the northern towns are "dry;" by law, the selling of alcohol is prohibited. Strange, although there isn't much for a tourist to do there, planeloads of them flew in several times a day for a quick "looky-loo."

We found the people of the town, fondly called "Tuk" by the locals, to be extremely friendly. Everyone smiled and said hello as we tramped the dusty streets. On returning from our first excursion into Tuk, we discovered a care package in the cockpit. At first we thought it was from one of the local people, but later discovered that it had been delivered by an acquaintance, Denny Synnot. He worked for the Institute of Ocean Sciences aboard the Coast Guard vessel, *Nahidik*, and was awaiting her arrival. Needless to say, we heartily enjoyed the feast of roast beef and fresh fruit.

The next day, Linda Cockney, who was in charge of water delivery, topped off our water tanks free of charge. In the evening, an Inuit couple, Frank and Nellie Pokiak, came aboard for a visit. They gave us some tasty, smoked, brine-soaked whitefish, enough for four meals. To me, Tuktoyaktuk was the place of many gifts.

During one of our many sight-seeing excursions, Winston and I visited an elderly Inuit lady who sewed the most beautiful parkas, hats,

Inuit whalebone and antler carving

mitts and slippers imaginable. Her furry rabbit and muskrat hats and seal- and moose-hide slippers were highlighted with handsome designs of intricate beadwork. Winston tried on a fur-trimmed parka which fit perfectly, but the price tag of $600 put it out of his reach.

Twenty-four hours of daylight take getting used to, especially when strolling the streets around two in the morning; small kids can be seen playing everywhere, and not in a quiet manner either. Many children, as well as adults, were curious about us and the boat. One evening, on my way back to the boat, I was surrounded by a bunch of inquisitive, sparkling-eyed Inuit girls intent on quizzing me about the boat. They asked questions such as: Is there a bathroom? a fridge? How many bedrooms? and more. They really wanted to see what *Dove* looked like inside, but since George and Winston were asleep, I had to refuse.

I also met several Inuit carvers busy in their studio near the airport. They allowed me to film them while they carved their soapstone creations. However, after a brief filming session, I gave it up because the extremely fine dust created by the whirring dremels almost blinded me and probably would have ruined the video camera. While browsing through my sketchbook, one of the most talented soapstone sculptors told me how difficult it was to get good quality drawing paper. I offered to give him an extra sketch pad I had brought along, but he insisted on a trade. I was more than happy to swap the pad for one of his fine art prints of a traditional Inuit hunter, spear in hand, standing over a seal's breathing hole.

Thursday, July 27
Still at Tuk. Waiting for the strong winds to ease up. We really should be moving; each passing day

makes the time frame more critical. The wind is cold; apparently Tuk has only had a couple of days of good summer weather. I hope winter doesn't come early.

Friday, July 28

Departed Tuktoyaktuk 0600. Unbelievable—we left port on a Friday despite Winston's superstition. Hope our luck doesn't change. Winds were light as we motored out of Kugmallit Bay into the Beaufort Sea. She made exceptionally good headway for most of the day. The khaki-colored Mackenzie River, flowing into the sea, pushed us along at an extra knot or two, with bursts of speed sometimes up to 11 knots. About four in the afternoon, *Dove* rounded Cape Bathurst, leaving the Beaufort Sea behind in favor of the teal-green waters of Amundsen Gulf.

On and off for the next few days, we saw what we believed were bowhead whales, their flukes and spumes of air and water clearly visible. Once, a large bowhead whale came nervously close to *Dove's* hull. I was so excited that I let go of the helm in search of my video camera, yelling, "George! Winston! Whales!" But by the time I reached the deck with my camera in hand, the leviathan had dived into the frigid depths, leaving only a ring of foam on the sea's surface. Although unable to capture the whale on film, I felt the rapture and excitement the whalers of old must have felt. Visions of Moby Dick, with a wild-eyed, maddened and determined Captain Ahab in pursuit, flashed before my eyes. At the helm, every time a whale came into view, I exclaimed under my breath like a kid, "Thar she blows!"

It took five days to motor from Tuk to Cambridge Bay, Victoria Island. At one point, with the wind blowing a favorable

10-15 knots, we attempted to sail in order to conserve fuel. Unfortunately, our speed dropped from 5 to 2-1/2 knots, forcing us to turn on the clamorous engine again.

The entire distance to Cambridge Bay was devoid of ice. But rocks? Winston drove *Dove* hard aground on a rock pile known as Simpson Rock just outside the entrance to Cambridge Bay. It was pretty scary as *Dove* rumbled and scraped across the ridge of boulders before grinding to a halt. The frigid, crystalline water revealed the large greenish-grey boulders on which *Dove* firmly stood. We had gone aground many times before, but usually, because the bottom was soft, we broke free quite easily. Simpson Rock proved more difficult. George hung off the rail and I from the ratlines, and after a lot of engine thrust, *Dove* eventually dragged herself free of the rock pile.

George wearing his ear protectors

CAMBRIDGE BAY

At four in the morning, August 12, we arrived at Cambridge Bay and moored to a well-maintained wharf, kitty-corner to the Coast Guard vessel, *Nahidik*. Since it was still early in the morning, we decided to get a little sleep before setting out to collect our mail and explore Cambridge Bay (Ikaluktutiak, "the fair fishing place.")

It had been raining at Cambridge Bay and, as we trudged the few short blocks to the Post Office, gobs of grey, cloggy mud stuck to our green rubber boots; my feet felt like lead. Even before the smiling post lady handed us our mail, I knew that one of the many letters was from Sandra. Hers always arrived in bright red envelopes, reminding me of a Valentine's Day card. Anxiously tearing it open, I felt as giddy as a teen-age boy with his first love. It's amazing how important mail becomes when you're far away from home and missing everyone who means so much.

After gathering our mail, Winston, George and I knocked on the door of Winston's friend, Chris Strube. I was surprised when it was opened by a tall, lean balding man with a full beard, twinkling eyes, and a compelling smile—wearing only a striped kimono and fur-trimmed slippers. Chris chuckled as he said, "Have a seat and make yourselves comfortable while I get dressed. Wouldn't want you guys to get any ideas looking at my hairy legs; after all, you've been away from home for a long time."

Later, as we sat around the kitchen table, relaxing and socializing over hot coffees, Chris asked, "How'd you guys like to go flying?" We leapt at the chance.

The flight across Victoria Island to the east coast was a delight to the eyes. I can well understand why the Inuit call their domain, Nunavut, "the beautiful land." From the air, the island looks like a slice of Swiss cheese, the holes filled with vivid shades of aquamarine water. The beaches look almost tropical, with the turquoise sea lapping the irregular shoreline. The water is so translucent that treacherous shoals and rocks lying beneath the surface could be seen clearly. The highlight of the flight was when Chris dove the small Cessna toward an unsuspecting herd of musk-ox leisurely grazing on the tundra. As the plane buzzed them, true to their nature, the shaggy-haired, curly-horned beasts scrambled to form a defensive circle. At the conclusion of the flight, Chris took us back to his home for a few home brews. What a treat!

During the evening, I enjoyed yet another ride; this time as a passenger on the back seat of an ATV driven by Denny Synnot who had rejoined Nahidik. Denny drove to the other side of the harbour where the old town site had been. Having been to Cambridge Bay many times, he wanted to show me some historical sites as well as introduce me to a famous Inuit carver who donates all the proceeds from his art toward helping the Inuit people and their environment.

Coast Guard vessel Nahidik

Amundsen's Maud, now derelict

The first site we came across was the wreck of the Maud, a small vessel used by Roald Amundsen, the first man to successfully traverse the Northwest Passage. Maud lies awash in a small cove, parts of her hull, deck and engine still visible. Until she sprang a leak, she was used by the Hudson's Bay Company as a floating warehouse.

On a hill overlooking the unfortunate Maud stood an abandoned church, built of grey stones; at the top of the spire, a stone cross sparkled in the sunlight like a miniature beacon. As we approached the little church, Our Lady of the Arctic, I imagined hymns, accompanied by an organ, wafting through the windows. Although the exterior appeared to be in excellent condition except for the roof, the interior was another story. It had been vandalized upstairs and down, the floors littered with debris and garbage. The stone church was built by the Oblate Missionaries during the early 1950s. Although no longer in use, it is under consideration for preservation. Hopefully, at some future time, the "little stone church" will once again be filled with joyous hymns and inspirational sermons.

On the other side of the church, at the bottom of a rocky incline, an abandoned mission boat was propped up close to the shoreline. Like the derelict *Maud*, the *Eagle* had seen better days. Although the badly-weathered hull was almost devoid of paint, the word *Eagle* lettered on each side of the bow and stern was still clearly legible. On close inspection, the wooden planks of the hull, deck and cabin were in sad shape, as was the engine. However, like the church with its glitter of life at the top of the cross, the *Eagle* possessed a spark of life. Sunlight streamed through one of the gaping portholes and glinted off a gearshift's shiny brass knob, no doubt used by many an imaginative boy pretending to be captain of the *Eagle*, no longer a mission boat, but terror of the high seas.

Once again astride the ATV, we headed toward a small white tent glistening in the sunlight, standing near the end of a rocky point that jutted into the sea. After what seemed a long, bone-jarring ride down a steep, shale-infested hill, we arrived at the sculptor's modest summer camp. Unfortunately, only his friendly, tail-wagging dog was home.

On the way back, Denny suddenly swerved off the road and headed for the top of a rocky hill saying, "There's something else I'd like to show you." As we crested the hill, what looked like a little man came into view. I was excited—this was one of the things I had hoped to see on our journey. Inuit legends say that such little stone men (inukshuk, "a silent messenger,") can steer a hunter to food or even save his life. If a person were to follow this inukshuk's gaze, he would eventually arrive at the Inuit sculptor's tent.

We spent a fair amount of time aboard *Nahidik*, relaxing over hot cups of tea and munching freshly-baked cookies. The captain, crew, and especially the two cooks, Bev and Kathy, were quite friendly toward us. One night, they smuggled a fabulous dinner aboard *Dove* and, no sooner had we eaten, than they returned with a six-pack of cold beer. Between Chris and the girls, this was the most beer we had enjoyed since the start of the trip despite the fact that Cambridge Bay, like the other northern communities, is "dry" of alcohol.

Trying not to miss any of the local sights, I visited "Many Pebbles" Municipal Golf Course which is unique because, instead of the usual green and manicured

lawns, the course is profusely strewn with boulders and stones. Only the area surrounding each hole is level and smooth, the cup marked by a thick wooden post. Chris told me, "There is no par. The winner is decided by who loses the least number of balls." Many Pebbles, more an obstacle course than a golf course, could well offer the world's most challenging golf game.

Three months to the day since leaving Nanaimo, we left the friendly arctic port of Cambridge Bay. Because of a positive ice report received from *Nahidik*, we had high hopes and eager expectations of quickly reaching our next destination—Gjoa Haven. The weather was gorgeous, on its best behavior, and everything was going as planned until—ice.

Around three in the morning, I was at the helm admiring a brilliant sunrise, with powder-puff clouds dipped in rouge and reflected on a silken sea. I noticed a long, bluish cloud formation stretching across the horizon. As *Dove* drew closer, I began to suspect that the cloud formation was a ridge of ice. However, not until the last moment could I be certain that it was ice, and I slowed *Dove*, cutting her hard to starboard to avoid certain collision.

The colors and patterns of the sky reflected on the sea can create illusions—a deadly illusion when combined with ice. I spent the remainder of my shift searching for a lead through the solid ridge of ice.

Four hours later, when I awoke to take my next shift, I was pleased to see that *Dove* was plowing through a sea completely free of ice. I said to Winston, "Great. You guys got through the ice. How much farther to Gjoa Haven?" A somewhat discouraged and downcast Winston replied, "We couldn't get through, so we're backtracking 40 kilometers to Jenny Lind Island to wait and see what happens with the ice."

JENNY LIND ISLAND

We used the parabolic radar antenna of an abandoned D.E.W. line station as a guide to steer *Dove* into Jenny Lind Bay. The sea looked tropical and inviting as the anchor plunged to the bottom of the clearest green water I had ever seen. However, the island's rocky shore slanted up gradually to a low, barren plain almost inundated by small shallow ponds. The boulder-strewn landscape appeared almost devoid of life and looked anything but inviting. When I finally had the time to explore some of the island, I was surprised at how much wildlife actually existed. A large variety of birds were evident and there were signs of musk-ox, caribou, rabbit, and fox.

It was great fun to poke about the many well-preserved buildings of the abandoned outpost. The main building resembled 20 mobile homes butted end to end, and looked as if it had housed about 100 military personnel. Listening to the moan of the wind, my footsteps echoing in the darkness of the long corridor, it felt spooky as I walked past many gaping doorways leading into blackness. Although most of the rooms were empty, we could still recognize the mess, laboratories, bedrooms, communications and, of course, the bar. Winston and I were able to climb inside the large fiberglass dome which seemed in relatively good condition, as did the other radar installations,

The only buildings not empty were five utility trailers

skidded onto the beach directly in front of *Dove*. Three of the trailers contained several roomettes with bunks, the other two were for recreation and cooking. I suspect that the trailer accommodations were used by work crews who periodically maintained the airstrip and other distant radar installations, apparently still operational.

During our explorations, we found a few eating utensils which we needed since one of us had inadvertently thrown some of ours overboard while doing dishes. Alongside the airstrip, we discovered a huge cache of aviation fuel, and a few barrels of diesel. What a bonus!

While Winston and I wandered around the island, the subject of sailing back home came up in our conversation. I said, "You shouldn't feel bad if the ice prevents us from going any further and we have to turn back. After all, it's still quite an accomplishment to have sailed this far."

Winston replied, "If we don't get through, then we're just three guys who happened to sail up here. We'll give it a couple of weeks to get through this end before I make the decision to sail back."

We spent two delightfully warm, sunny days relaxing and exploring Jenny Lind Island before *Dove* was once again on her way to Gjoa Haven. Five hours later, the ice stopped us cold, almost 3 km sooner than before. There was nothing to do but return to Jenny Lind Island.

August 11

If I have learned anything during this voyage, it is that I am truly out of my element here. This sea and land of the Arctic, although called Canada, is not like any Canada I have ever known. In my opinion, the people and wildlife indigenous to this region should be allowed to live and rule here without the so-called meaningful meddling of government and business. This area of the world belongs to them, and only them, because they alone are able to exist in complete harmony and sympathy with the harshness of the arctic environment.

August 12th turned out to be a devastating and depressing day for me. I enjoyed most of the day ashore, sketching, photographing, and filming some of the sights around the installation, including a rather comical episode featuring Winston and me bathing and washing our clothes. After dinner, I returned ashore to do some more filming. All went well until time to return. If I've climbed into a dinghy once, I've climbed into one a

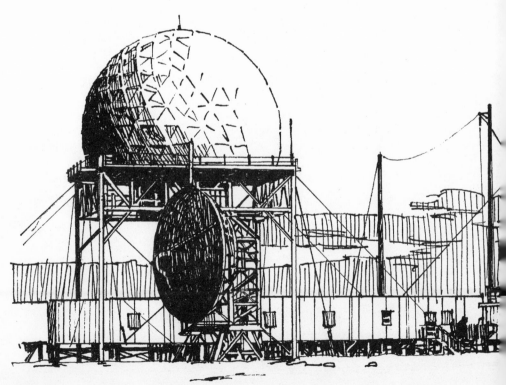

thousand times. However, it takes only one clumsy incident to ruin a whole day. While attempting to launch the dinghy into the rolling surf, I almost swamped it. The erratic, violent motion sent the video camera, usually in a waterproof case, sliding along the back seat into the sea. Although I managed to grab it almost instantly, the momentary submersion proved fatal. I wondered if Winston's superstition about leaving port on a Friday had anything to do with it.

Since the film of the comical segment with Winston and me was lost in the dinghy mishap, I attempted to record it in writing:

The Goose Shit Dip'n'Rinse

It was a warm, hazy afternoon with a slight, cool breeze blowing off the sea. George, Winston and I had just returned to the dinghy after a leisurely

stroll to where a river flowed into the far end of the bay. Since we were hot and sticky with sweat, Winston and I decided to wash ourselves and our long red underwear. George, more concerned about getting a drink and, probably, filling his belly, returned to the boat.

Winston and I rooted about the trailer containing kitchen paraphernalia until we found two large, black plastic garbage bags, a box of powdered Spic'n'Span floor cleaner, three large stainless steel bowls, and one well-used bar of soap. We filled the plastic bags with water from a large puddle nearby, careful not to disturb the goose droppings and some sort of brown, slimy vegetation clinging to the bottom of the puddle. We secured the bags with a scavenged shoelace and left them in the sun to warm the water. We retired to the comfort of the bar trailer where we lounged on the couch and easy chair, talking about home, the trip, and the possibility of being forced to leave *Dove* for the winter. We also joked about how it would be nice to have a cold beer, but the fridge in the corner was empty.

Checking the temperature of the water, I noticed George rowing back. By the time he arrived, the bags of water felt warm and we filled the stainless bowls, eager to wash ourselves. George refused to participate in the Goose Shit Dip'n'Rinse, and chuckled while we gingerly stripped. I, too, laughed as Winston, wearing a scanty pair of maroon gauchies [undershorts] and green rubber boots, wincingly applied the tepid water to his face and body. Stripping to my birthday suit, sharp little stones digging into my tender tootsies, I began the famous "Lenny two-step." Because we were on camera, I tied a shirt around my waist, but couldn't resist a moon. (No wonder the camera took a dive.) Brrr—the water felt cold.

After hanging our long johns to dry, I wondered if we or the underwear were really clean. Scrubbing with floor cleaner and rinsing with goose-shit-contaminated water didn't seem the ideal cleaning combination. Although refreshed, I still had a nagging feeling that, at any time, my body could break out with some disgusting disease such as: "goose-dip shititis," "gooey goose pimples," or the dreaded "goosey down syndrome." So far, every-thing feels fine, but I'm a little concerned about the two large bumps which have just emerged on my back. Oh well, time will tell.

During our stay at Jenny Lind, I managed to complete a poem I'd been writing since the beginning of the Northwest Passage.

Voyage of the Northwest Passage

Beneath a cover of soft grey clouds,
its underbelly glinting of alabaster
from a tired old sun,
the wings of a southward gull
flash soft, silent shadows along its underside.
Oh—to be that gull,
light-feathered friend of sea and sky;
to fly from these ice-packed, arctic seas
across the gravel, permafrost tundra,
o'er lofty, craggy mountain tops
to a land and sea more gentle,

where trees, with chatterbox leaves,
whisper gently in my lady's ear.
But alas, I'm no bird of any kind;
I am but a man, a sailor man;
a daytime, nighttime dreamer
who stands his trick at the helm
awaiting a barrage of brutal bergs;
the lethal ice of winter
and a thousand winters before
that block the voyage of the Northwest Passage,
where men of Franklin's ilk lie, bone bare—
truth testament to the Titan ice—
and the howl of the freezing banshee wind.

The day before we left Jenny Lind, Winston and I took one last hike to the abandoned station. We spotted a caribou (tuctu) about 275 meters off the gravel road. With a full crown of antlers, it stood silhouetted against the sky like a household ornament. The animal warily watched our approach but, instead of running off as we might expect, it began to walk slowly toward us. The caribou seemed amazingly inquisitive and came within 90 meters before stopping. As we stood staring in awe, it turned suddenly, white tail flashing in the sunlight, and nonchalantly ambled off, occasionally looking back over its shoulder until it blended, then vanished, into the earth-toned landscape.

I felt fortunate to have beheld such an animal at a close distance. I'm not sure if the caribou felt the same, but it should have been more cautious. We could easily have been two armed Inuit hunters in search of food. Experiencing simple things—the majesty of the caribou, a glimpse of a small animal scurrying for cover, the glint of sunlight on a wildflower's petal, sparkling ice on a smooth sea, or the bleached bones of an animal—were more rewarding for me than the actual voyage through the Northwest Passage.

We sailed from Jenny Lind Island on Monday, August 14, at three in the morning. The day was sunny and virtually wind free. Although before, on our earlier attempts to leave Jenny Lind, the ice pack halted our progress and raised the possibility of abandoning the idea of completing the Northwest Passage in one season, the ice had now vanished, leaving only tiny reminders of its previous existence.

Evening found *Dove* quietly at anchor a little southeast of Cape John Herschel, off Petersen Island. A red beacon blatantly blinked in front of another abandoned D.E.W. site; a group of sea lions, noses

A family of sea lions

Winston at the helm

in the air, ignored our presence. While Winston and George snoozed below, I enjoyed the solitude on deck and the splendor of a spectacular sunset. My hopes rose.

There was no real darkness, so first light came almost immediately as we headed for Gjoa Haven with Winston at the helm. Almost exactly 24 hours after leaving Jenny Lind Island, we arrived at Gjoa Haven. Luckily, and to our amazement, the bay that had been completely frozen over the day before now contained only a few chucks of ice on their way out with the tide.

Through Infamous Bellot Strait to Pond Inlet

Gjoa Haven was called the "finest little harbour in the world" by Roald Amundsen. He named this sheltered harbour after his little ship, *Gjoa,* in which, around the turn of the century, he spent two years in this area delineating the exact location of the North Magnetic Pole. Not to be confused with the North Pole, the North Magnetic Pole is the place to which the compass points. Since Amundsen's time, the North Magnetic Pole, which continually moves northwards in a wobbling, circular manner, has moved over 640 kilometers, well away from where Amundsen first pin-pointed it on King William Island. It is now close to Resolute Bay on Cornwallis Island.

An earlier explorer of this region was Sir John Franklin. In 1845, he sailed in search of the Northwest Passage with two well-equipped ships and 129 men. By 1848, it became apparent that both *Erebus* and *Terror* were lost. Searches made in the latter half of the 19th century turned up assorted artifacts and several graves, but the events that put an end to the expedition were unknown.

Beginning in 1981, intensive searches under the direction of Owen Beattie were renewed and traces of the Franklin party were found at numerous sites. As more evidence was assembled, the picture of the events became clearer and are described in Beattie's book, *Frozen in Time.* Beattie believed that the remaining survivors died on King William Island in 1848.

The first vessel to navigate the Northwest Passage in both

directions was the R.C.M.P. schooner, St. Roch, under the command of Sgt. Henry Larsen, who stopped at Gjoa Haven on August 27, 1941. Many people of the north, including some at Gjoa Haven, still remember Larsen; his reputation remains admirable.

Gjoa Haven was similar to the other settlements we had visited. I roamed in search of subjects to photograph and sketch. The short houses on stilts, rising from the beaches to the hills overlooking the harbour, appeared to be built from the same kits as the houses in Cambridge

Bay and Tuktoyaktuk. The roads that wound through the hamlet were sandier. The whole of Gjoa Haven seemed neater, the people more easy-going. Perhaps because of the dearth of paying jobs and commercial enterprise, it's not such a busy place. Although the Inuit still maintain their old traditions of hunting and fishing, many earn their livings by carving beautiful sculptures or jewelry from soapstone, antlers and bone.

Most of the Inuit people I met had been kind and courteous; Gjoa Haven was no exception. Although many of them were outgoing, some were much like me, shy. Young children seemed to take great delight in my appearance. Because of my curly white hair and beard and my red coat, they often asked if I was Santa Claus.

As I sketched a couple of pre-school kids playing on the beach in front of *Dove*, they told me, "We thought you were a woman." We had quite a giggle when I retorted, "A woman? When was the last time you saw a bearded lady?" Santa Claus, Popeye, that I could understand; but a woman?

During our short stay, we were befriended by a tall, handsome swarthy man named Axel. It turned out he was not only the manager of the Kekertak Cooperative (a large general store), but the newly-built Amundsen Hotel as well. He generously gave us the use of a $250/day hotel suite consisting of a living room/kitchen, bedroom and bathroom. It seemed elegant and luxurious after living aboard *Dove* so long. But, as odd as it may seem, we never really made use of the suite except for the bathtub. I felt indescribably decadent as I lay back and soaked in the deep hot water, then drifted off to sleep.

Since I have an avid interest in art, Axel took me to the home of world-renowned soapstone sculptor, Judas Ullulaq. As we waited at his door, my eyes wandered across his yard to a simple work table with an irregular piece of plywood for a top and various articles of junk constituting the legs. Scattered about the work area were a few objets d'art in various stages of completion. Everything, including the entire yard, was covered with a fine white powdery dust, as if a light snow had fallen on Judas' domain.

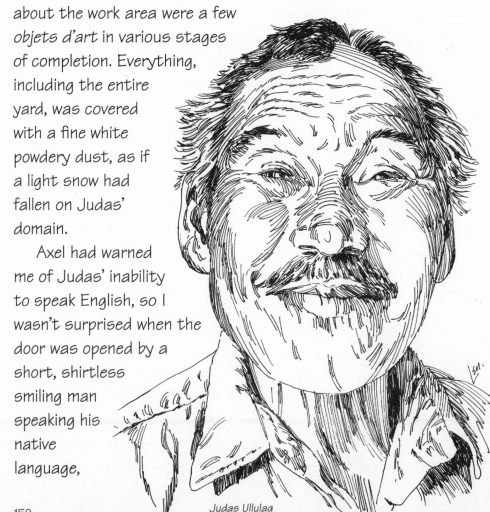

Axel had warned me of Judas' inability to speak English, so I wasn't surprised when the door was opened by a short, shirtless smiling man speaking his native language,

152

Judas Ullulaq

Inuktutuk. Entering Judas' modest home, I saw that we had interrupted his lunch; two half-eaten frozen dinners sat on the kitchen table. We asked if we should come back a little later, but he wouldn't hear of it, gesturing for us to sit on the couch. Axel, a very busy man, had things to do and politely excused himself, leaving me alone with Judas and his young teen-age grandson, Samuel, who translated our conversation.

A proud but simple man, Judas took great delight describing some photographs pinned to the wall. They were mostly of him and his family when he was younger. He motioned to some awards he'd received for his artwork, but made certain I was aware of an award his grandson had earned playing hockey.

On the floor stood "The Dancing Musk-ox," a large, green soapstone sculpture of a musk-ox with ivory horns that Judas had just completed. While snapping a few slides of Judas and Samuel, I stepped back and inadvertently knocked over the sculpture. I watched with trepidation as it thundered across the floor, losing its ivory horns. I thought my clumsiness had destroyed his wonderful sculpture, but the ever-smiling Judas reassured me. "Don't worry, it's made of stone, you can't break it." Still, I felt like a klutz as I watched him deftly refasten the horns.

On my way out, Judas showed me a load of arctic char he had just caught. He seemed more pleased with his full freezer of fish than with his awards. It was refreshing to see that some-one who has had one-man art exhibitions in Washington, D.C., Tokyo, and other world centers doesn't possess an overblown ego. Unlike many people, possessions and self-importance were of no concern to this man. I—and a great many people—could take lessons from Judas Ullulaq.

In search of a copy of the Inuit alphabet, Winston and I met Frieda Maaskant, a teacher at the local school. She invited us to her home for a delicious spaghetti dinner, with succulent salad, warm, buttered garlic bread, and chilled wine. She had also invited two teacher friends, Ron and Bonnie, and the conversation was stimulating. When asked to read one of my poems, I felt as if I was back in school being graded for grammar, poetic construction, and creativity. I was a little intimidated, as well as embarrassed.

Immediately after leaving Frieda's house, I called home to tell Sandra we were leaving Gjoa Haven in the morning for Pond Inlet, our next stop. I was upset when she said that she had borrowed money from her mother to make ends meet. As the three of us headed back to the boat, Winston talked about taking a week or two to prepare *Dove* for the winter in the event we might have to leave her. For the life of me, I couldn't understand how it would take three people a week or two to prepare an eight and a half meter sailboat for the winter. Winston and George also wanted to stay two or three days in Ottawa to sightsee.

With the recent loss of my $2,500 video camera, Sandra's

Frieda Maaskant

154

depleted finances, and being just plain broke, I blew my stack. I felt obligated to return home as soon as it was possible. Talking about two weeks to ready *Dove* seemed way out of line, especially since I would have to borrow money for the flight home.

I blurted out, "I'm outta here on the first available flight when this journey comes to an end, so that should give you some incentive to get everything done real soon."

An upset Winston replied, "Then you better just hit the road, 'cause I don't have time to argue with you!" George just chuckled.

Needless to say, the row back to the boat was unusually quiet. The next morning, just before we raised anchor, I apologized to Winston. "I'm sorry for what I said last night. Of course I'll stay until the boat is looked after."

Under a warm but cloudy sky, we departed the sheltered harbour of Gjoa Haven on August 17 at seven in the morning. The sea was calm as Winston nosed *Dove* into Rasmussen Basin and headed her almost due north toward Rae Strait. The previous night's episode was settled, but not forgotten.

About four hours later, the sky was still grey, the sea was grey, and I, too, felt a little grey. As *Dove* sliced her way through Rae Strait, I scanned the horizon in search of a beacon marked on the chart. I saw what looked like a tree although I knew it couldn't possibly be one, there are no trees in this part of the world. I hollered down to Winston, "I see something up ahead. It looks like a tree."

Winston quickly scurried from his bunk to take a look. He said, "That's no tree; it's probably that Croatian sailboat that's been stuck in the ice somewhere up here."

Sure enough, as *Dove* drew near, the tree turned out to be the two-masted Croatian ketch, *Hrvatska Cigra* (Croatian Tern).

Dove meets the Croatian Tern

Dove was rafted securely alongside and we were invited aboard for a tour by Mladen Sutej, captain and leader of the expedition.

The Croatian Tern, approximately three times the size of *Dove*, had all the bells and whistles imaginable. The electronic equipment alone consisted of two independent GPS systems, digital world maps, a 48-kilometer range radar, various instruments for controlling the vessel's speed and list and for checking direction and wind speed. All this plus several radios, including a VHF instrument of 25W and a short-wave amateur station of 100W with an automatic tuner. Besides an inflatable runabout, *Croatian Tern* was equipped with a 12-person survival raft and an inflatable boat with attached motor-driven delta hang glider for reconnaissance from the air. In comparison, *Dove* looked like "rub-a-dub-dub, three men in a tub."

I watched *Croatian Tern* slowly dip beneath the horizon and thought about their voyage to circumnavigate North and South America, going as far south as Antarctica. I wished them all the best in their quest. Although the Croatian vessel was a larger, more sophisticated and comfortable boat, I still preferred *Dove*. If I was envious of anything, it was their budget; more money would have been nice.

Friday, August 18, 1100 hours

Near Cape Alexander, Larsen Sound. The ice report from two days ago shows about six-tenths ice coverage, but thankfully it is more like two-tenths. The *Croatian Tern* broke free yesterday, after being trapped by the ice for two weeks at Fort Ross on the east side of Bellot Strait. Since they had no further problems, I feel confident it will be the same for us. The only difficulties I can foresee are possible changes in weather and wind. Although much of the ice has either melted or drifted off, the main body of pack ice can be seen clearly off to the west. So far, the weather today is gorgeous, sunny with a slight breeze.

Later the same day:

At the moment, *Dove* is fast approaching Bellot Strait, a narrow cut which slices between the Boothia Peninsula, North America's most northerly point, and Somerset Island. It is noted in the *Arctic Pilot Book* as being extremely dangerous due to the 9-knot current. As if that isn't bad enough, a whole lot of bergs might be swirling around in the whirlpools. I'm hoping we'll arrive at slack tide and be ice free.

Saturday, August 19, 1405 hours

Rubbing my eyes after a somewhat fitful sleep,
I again took my shift at the helm. The sun, hard
on the nose and slightly above the horizon, glared
into my eyes. To escape its brilliance, I cautiously
peeked around either side of the mast in order to
steer a safe course between the bergs languishing
on the placid sea. Fortunately, there weren't many;
instead, most of my shift was spent dodging the
sun's vicious blaze.

Shortly after I finished my shift, the ice gathered forces with a
vengeance; it took the three of us to work the boat up to the
mouth of the infamous Bellot Strait. As *Dove* cautiously
approached the gaping maw, I began to conjure visions in my
mind, terrifying images of a turbulent current churning
monstrous bergs in the whirlpools that lay below the steep,
treacherous cliffs. To my surprise and awe, big, bad Bellot Strait
was on its best behavior. A few small bergs lolled about the
entrance. I thought, it's a trick, they're just waiting to pounce
on us like a patient puma. But all went well; *Dove*
chugged on by the bergs that spun slowly in the
eddies awaiting the tide change.

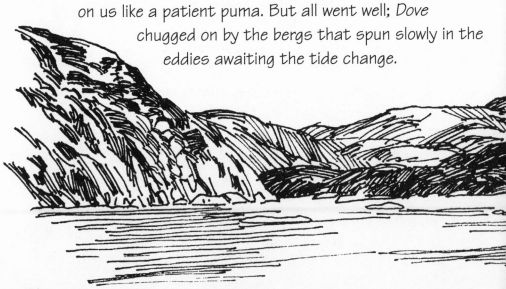

As *Dove* slid slowly by Magpie Rock and on to the eastern side of the strait, past Brands Island, I though how lucky we were to have made a safe and uneventful passage of Bellot Strait. St. Roch's struggle through the strait had been far more of a challenge.

> The strait was clear of ice, but in the middle there was a barrier right across, held there by some heavy grounded ice. The strait is only half a mile wide   and there's a terrible current. As the ice came pouring in behind us, there was nothing else to do but crash into it and attempt to drift through. This we did; the strong current causing large whirlpools in which large cakes of ice spun and gyrated. Many times we thought the ship would crack like a nut under the pressure. Sometimes we became stationary off projecting points of land—high, dark   inaccessible cliffs—the strait is about 18 miles long.
>
> We had two young Eskimos aboard, a man and his wife. One has to admire the quality of these people. At times when things looked really bad they would go up on the forecastle head and sing at the top of their voices. They told me they were singing so the ship wouldn't get crushed, so I told them to keep on singing. They were quite pleased after we got through, when I told them their singing had

Bellot Strait

no doubt helped us a great deal. Meanwhile the people at the eastern end of the strait, at Hudson's Bay Company post, Fort Ross, had anxiously watched our struggles, and they all came swarming aboard to welcome us.

The Famous Voyages of the Royal Canadian Mounted Police Schooner, St. Roch by Sergeant Henry Larsen (F.R.G.S.)

After passing the southern tip of Long Island, I looked through the binoculars toward Depot Bay and could see clearly two small buildings located on Somerset Island—the abandoned Fort Ross mentioned by Sgt. Henry Larsen. It was hard to imagine what life had been like at this forlorn outpost, in such a bleak and desolate location so far from a friendly, civilized community. I was seeing the "arctic paradise" with its best disposition; winter conditions were totally beyond my conception.

August 19

We toasted our completion of the Northwest Passage with rum flavored with Tang (orange crystals), and a handful of potato chips; this is hardly a champagne and caviar voyage. We may have been premature with our celebration; I wasn't sure if the entrance to Lancaster Sound or Pond Inlet marked the end of the passage, but I felt confident we would reach our destination. Winston has just informed me there is a lot of ice up ahead. I hope this is not a bad omen.

Bad news—bad ice. Perhaps I should have had a nap, I could be up all night fending off the ice. The ice chart we were given at Gjoa Haven showed this area to be clear; so much for space-age technology. As usual, the ice has proven its unpredictability.

Since we figured the worst of the journey was behind us, I felt as though we were finally on our way home. During my shifts at the helm yesterday, a poem came to mind:

Homeward Bound

The sea that lies before me
is as flat as calm can be,
not a ripple nor a wave
undulating do I see.

The gull that flies o'er my head
in a sky the hue of lead,
lifts a wing to cast a wave
before soaring on ahead.

The lass who cries her heart out
for the one who sails about,
blew a kiss, a silent wave,
she's the one for me—no doubt.

The sea still lies before me
where the gull is flying free;
not too long before I wave
to the lass who waits for me.

Sunday, August 20, 0640 hours

For the past three hours we've been battling with the ice in Prince Regent Inlet just off Somerset Island; the Brodeur peninsula is clearly visible about 24 km to the east. The ice floes are thinning out but the surface of the sea is covered with a slight

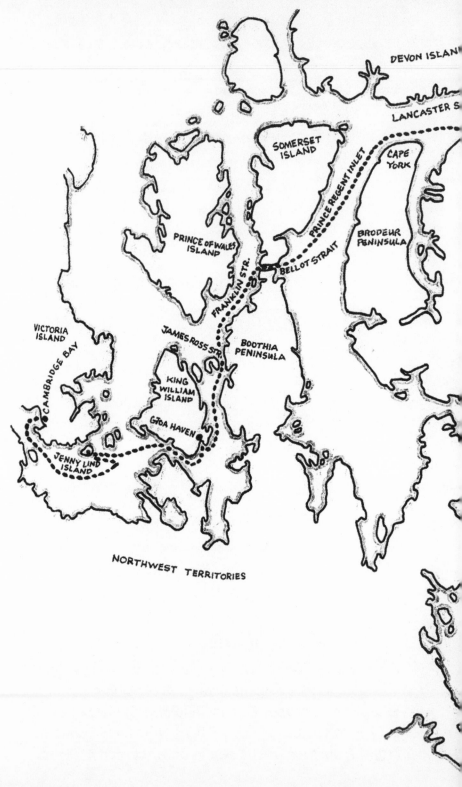

DEVON ISLAND

LANCASTER S.

SOMERSET ISLAND

CAPE YORK

PRINCE REGENT INLET

BRODEUR PENINSULA

PRINCE OF WALES ISLAND

BELLOT STRAIT

FRANKLIN STR.

VICTORIA ISLAND

JAMES ROSS STR.

BOOTHIA PENINSULA

CAMBRIDGE BAY

KING WILLIAM ISLAND

GJOA HAVEN

JENNY LIND ISLAND

NORTHWEST TERRITORIES

SOUND

BYLOT ISLAND

BAFFIN BAY

POND INLET

N

BAFFIN ISLAND

CLYDE RIVER

GREENLAND

DAVIS STRAIT

PANGNIRTUNG

CUMBERLAND SOUND

skim of ice. Easy to see how winter roars in without remorse, freezing everything solid in a short time. Strange, there have been times at home when I almost scalded my hands doing dishes—now they get numb from icy-cold seawater.

August 20, 1720 hours

Squinting into the distance, I saw a thick ridge of ice; we were in the thick of it in 30 minutes. Carefully, still under full power, I edged *Dove* through the skinny leads until the maze of ice forced me to cut the engine to half-throttle; both Winston and George came to investigate the problem. A disgruntled George muttered incessantly about how the ice chart had showed no ice in the vicinity. Later, Winston grumbled something about the ice and that I was a jinx. Me? I just smiled to myself and thought, ice will be ice.

I tend to look at an iceberg as if it were a sailboat; the part showing above the water is the sail and the part below, the keel. Unlike a sailboat, there's no pilot to steer the ice, so when wind, tide and current come into play, there is usually one hell of a traffic jam.

Later in the afternoon, the sea was mostly free of ice and I thought of home and Sandra's upcoming birthday on the 23rd. I was looking forward to phoning her from Pond Inlet, about 40 hours away. Unable to buy her a birthday gift, I decided to make her a card, one that would put a smile on her face and a giggle in her heart.

My Long-legged Girl

A hippo from Fantasia
or a Madame of Eurasia
dressed in nothing but a tutu
may be some kind of lulu;
but when it comes to dancing
or searing hot romancing,
then there's nothing in the world
like my long-legged girl.

Now Clyde loved his Bonnie goil
and Popeye, his Olive Oyle,
plus Julie and her Romeo
like Anthony and his Cleo;
but when it comes to lovers
underneath the bedroom covers,
then there's no one in the world
like my long-legged girl.

In the late afternoon, *Dove* rounded Cape York, Brodeur Peninsula, and nosed her way into Lancaster Sound. The barometer began to fall, dark ominous clouds gathered and a cold northwesterly wind came up. Each time I took my turn at the helm, the wind was stronger and the clouds more menacing, until around the midnight hour, *Dove* and her companions were again tested by the ravaging force of an arctic gale. The winds blew straight up our stern as we took our turns navigating the boat through a belligerent, steep, white-capped sea. *Dove's* average speed of 5-6 knots was enhanced by the gale's steady 7 or 8 knots and an occasional 9- to 11-knot adrenaline rush.

Steering *Dove* through the erratic waves was exciting at times, calling for creative navigating. It was scary as we descended into the treacherous troughs towering over *Dove*, and I was afraid of being forced broadside and broached by a rogue wave. That the results could be disastrous was ever on my mind. After many hours of battling maddened Lancaster Sound, we reached our most northerly position, approximately 73° North, turned *Dove* , and finally began our southward journey.

Our introduction to the first behemoth of an iceberg occurred soon after we entered Navy Board Inlet.

Monday, August 21

As the iceberg began to top the horizon, it looked like one of the cruise ships we had seen back in May while sailing the Inside Passage to Prince Rupert. The giant berg seemed to take forever to climb over the horizon; when we drew alongside, I felt fragile, small and insignificant.

The iceberg's height was in excess of 40 meters and it glistened and sparkled like a cathedral-sized diamond; the power it exuded was magnetic. I watched in awe as the behemoth casually parted the pounding waves on its journey toward Davis Strait; there, after a journey of 1,000 or more kilometers, it would eventually melt and become one with the sea.

August 21, 1452 hours

At this very moment, *Dove* is pushing her way through the heavy whitecaps of Navy Board Inlet that separates Borden Peninsula on Baffin Island from Bylot Island. The flat-topped, brownish-grey mountains on Bylot Island are in stark contrast to the moody blue, glacier-covered mountains of the Borden Peninsula. We passed several more icebergs, but none as large or as spectacular as that first giant.

ALBERT HARBOUR

Arrived Pond Inlet; wind is blowing too hard to
anchor safely.

Since anchoring was out of the question, Winston thought of
securing *Dove* to the stern of the large freighter, *Arctic Viking*,
which was anchored in front of Pond Inlet. But after mulling over
the idea, with the cold wind blowing in our tired faces, Winston
decided to bypass Pond Inlet in favor of a sheltered anchorage
16 kilometers to the west. We hoped the strong winds would
abate by morning so we could return to Pond Inlet for our mail
and some fuel.

An hour and a half later, we found ourselves surrounded by
barren, shale-covered mountains rising sharply from the sea to
an altitude of about 600 meters. We dropped the hook into the
placid water of Albert Harbour directly in front of a small, inviting beach. An occasional wild gust of wind blasted down from
the mountain tops; one gust was so powerful that the anchor
was dislodged, momentarily setting *Dove* adrift.

I longed to go ashore and explore the immediate area, but
my bed looked far more enticing. However, after a good, sound
power nap and a bite to eat, I was on my way.

August 22, later

I discovered a boulder-jammed stream, sometimes
trickling, sometimes cascading, that wound down
between two mountains and emptied into the bay.
The stream, probably fed by a glacier, was so-o-o
cold and tasted so-o-o good I could hardly stop
drinking. Beside the stream, many hardy flowers

grew in what little soil clung desperately to the beach. Over the years, Inuit hunters must have used this location; I discovered several old campfire rings and a couple of rusty leghold animal traps.

I hate the continual motoring; the engine noise is extremely loud. I would have enjoyed the exploration more, but when the babbling of a stream is barely audible over the ringing in my ears, my pleasure is diminished.

Due to the strong prevailing winds, we were forced to stay another day at Albert Harbour. I spent much of my time drawing up some personalized postcards to send to relatives, friends and sponsors. Later, the three of us went ashore and built a cairn in homage to the people who gave us money and encouragement during our presentation at the Nanaimo Boat Show. We sealed the guest book containing their names and comments in a waterproof container and placed it beneath our squat little pile of stones. As if to pacify the arctic gods, Winston fulfilled a request from an Australian buddy and set the friend's old worn-out jacket ablaze. The cairn looked like a funeral pyre burning in the autumn dusk.

I wondered how long it would be before someone discovered the contents of the cairn. What if the container was found by a weary Inuit in need of a little warmth? Perhaps we should have thrown in a book of matches along with the papers.

Wednesday, August 23

It snowed last night around the 300-meter elevation. Just a puff to let us know—or warn us— that winter is not far off.

The following morning, we hoisted the anchor and headed *Dove* toward the narrow exit of Eclipse Sound. I noticed that snow had fallen again, this time a little lower and heavier. By the time we returned to Pond Inlet, the wind had died considerably.

Clyde River
Befriended by the R.C.M.P.

POND INLET

As the anchor dropped into the gentle swell, two huge icebergs drifted slowly by on the starboard side. Pond Inlet looked like a bleak place from the sea; hard to understand why anyone would voluntarily live there, other than those born to it. Once I climbed the hills and walked the streets looking out toward the sea, I saw that the view was anything but bleak; it was absolutely breathtaking. The snow-covered mountains across the inlet on Bylot Island rise steeply—almost 2,000 meters—from the icy blue sea, and stand tall and erect like guardians of the north. An armada of stately icebergs sailed silently through the inlet.

Pond Inlet (Mittimatalik, "where birds can be seen resting or sitting") is also referred to as Purtujuk, "land with depth." Archeological evidence suggests that it

is the most ancient of Inuit campsites in the Canadian Arctic. The small hamlet has a population of about 850 people and, like other northern communities, alcohol is controlled here.

The people were most enjoyable, especially the children. I had a lot of fun photographing them in their daily activities, mainly playing. Some took great delight in performing and making funny faces for the camera, while others simply stood and smiled.

On a cliff looking out to sea stood a sod house (qarmaq), a traditional Inuit home. Houses such as these were used as recently as the 1960s. This one was erected in 1991 as a tourist attraction. When I opened the door, I realized someone was living there and could return any moment, and I felt like an intruder.

Another prominent attraction was a life-sized crucifix erected high on a hill overlooking Pond Inlet. Two ravens flew overhead, black against the sky, as I stood looking at Jesus nailed to the cross, wondering if this was anything like the actual setting of his crucifixion. He looked quite peaceful beneath his crown of thorns, but what a terrible way to die, especially for the Son of God. Hard to believe that a man as compassionate as Jesus could come to such a violent, torturous end.

We phoned home, had our passports stamped, collected our

mail, and reprovi-
sioned the boat,
then headed back to
Albert Harbour for the night. I
watched from the stern until the crucifix
high on the hill was no longer visible and
Pond Inlet merged into the background.

Friday, August 25

Departed Albert Harbour 0300. The
morning was calm, no wind whatsoever.
Sunny and warm with some cloud cover
beyond the horizon. It feels good to be going
home and yet, as I watch the majestic scenery
go by and realize I will never see this high arctic
region again, I feel that a little piece of me will be
left behind.

Looking back from a future time, this arctic journey on a small
sailboat will undoubtedly be one of the highlights of my life.
Although at times I've bitched and complained, mainly to the
little person that lives inside my head, I appreciate the fact
that Winston allowed me to crew for him; without his tireless
effort and push, this voyage would never have taken place and
I would have missed an experience of a lifetime.

During the afternoon, I kept smelling a rather ripe aroma.
Checking my body, especially the armpit area, I realized—yup—
it was me. Since no shower facilities existed on board, what was
a body to do? I decided to wash myself with cold seawater.

A few gusts of cool air whipped about me as I began to shed
my clothes in the cockpit. Despite the breeze, it felt good to
stand with the warm sun shining on my nakedness. Dipping the

washrag into the freezing, soapy water, I gingerly began to wash my body, starting with my feet. The cold water almost took my breath away as I scrubbed my chest and armpits, not to mention more private areas. As the cool breeze caressed my quivering body, I broke into a multitude of goose bumps. My feet were still a little numb an hour later, but I felt clean and completely refreshed.

Later, Winston received a call from a passing Coast Guard vessel, congratulating him on our success in sailing the Northwest Passage. It is a pity that the government is drastically downsizing the Coast Guard and the many lighthouses located along Canada's extensive and rugged coastline. With ever-advancing computer and robotic technology, they seem to be going the way of the dinosaur. I suspect many of the vessels and lighthouses are armed with the latest computer equipment for combating all navigational hazards, but God help us if the power is ever switched off.

At first, Davis Strait appeared as if it would be a cake-run, since the latest ice chart showed little or no ice along the Baffin Island coastline. We passed quite a few icebergs and some pack ice, but not enough to hinder our progress. We hoped that the winds of a few days earlier had blown out the ice, but it was not to be.

Saturday, August 26

Started out well; sea calm, a few dark clouds approaching from the southeast. As *Dove* drew closer to the clouds, the sea began to ripple until, before long, it was as rough as the Bering Sea. When I took over my watch at 2300, *Dove* was encompassed by a heavy fog, visibility about 90 meters.

I had heard Winston describe how he had once steered *Dove* in a complete circle without realizing it. I remember laughing to myself because our seafaring commander hadn't held a course; when I took my turn at the helm, I began to understand.

Winston

Before me in the dark fog loomed an iceberg the size of a six-floor apartment building. Trying to cope with the thrashing sea, a mind-of-its-own compass, and the wildly gyrating needle on the GPS, I found myself in deep trouble. During the time it took me to glance from the compass to the GPS, I lost sight of the iceberg—a large and dangerous iceberg.

In a panic state, hoping *Dove* had already passed the iceberg, I threw open the tinted portside window for better visibility. No, not there. I quickly opened the starboard window. It wasn't there either! How the hell *do* you lose an iceberg? Squinting into the fog, not knowing which direction to steer, I was bloody scared. The elusive berg finally emerged out of the mist on the starboard side and I realized in horror that I, too, had steered little *Dove* in a complete circle—around an iceberg, no less. Perhaps subconsciously aware of the dilemma, Winston appeared from the darkness below to take charge of the situation. I trembled with anxiety until *Dove* was safely on course again.

Once more in control, I kept my eyes on the foggy conditions ahead and the red glare of the compass, making sure *Dove* never went 10 degrees either side of the designated course. With the coming daylight, visibility seemed easier. However, a tired Lenny was happy when George arrived to relieve him.

During my next shift, as the boat pounded into the wind and waves, what looked like an ordinary, gale-driven wave turned out to be anything but. *Dove* crested the oncoming wave and the bottom suddenly fell out. Airborne for a moment, she slammed down hard and loud, sending a shudder through the length of her hull. Fortunately, there was no ice in the trough or the outcome might have been different.

It was a long night, one of the worst since the voyage began. The gale didn't let up for a minute, and I found myself hugging the toilet. What made matters worse was the dense fog and the fact that the compass wasn't working properly due to the pull of magnetic north. Add darkness and throw in a few icebergs, and sailing Davis Strait became uncomfortable and dangerous.

After my last shift, I remember crawling onto George's bunk, securing myself in the confines of the lee cloth, and listening to the pounding and gurgling noises reverberating through *Dove's* hull. I don't recall falling asleep, but when I awoke from a lulling dream, *Dove* was moving along in an unusual manner—smoothly. For a moment I thought I was still asleep and dreaming, until I looked out and saw the small hamlet of Clyde River sparkling in the sunshine under what looked like a halo of fog.

CLYDE RIVER

Sunday, August 27

Arrived Clyde River 0500. After eating a large bowl of mush for breakfast, I accompanied Winston to church. Since I never go to church, I asked myself, why the sudden interest? I wasn't going to ask for help or safe journey; maybe it was what Winston had said earlier, "I've had a lot of luck in my lifetime and it doesn't hurt to say, 'Thanks.'" So that's what I did. I said, "Thanks."

We attended the Church of the Redeemer (Anglican). The congregation was mostly Inuit, and the service was almost entirely in Inuktitut. Attendance was very casual; children did pretty much as they pleased but were, for the most part, well-behaved and quiet except for an occasional crying infant tucked deep inside an amautik (jacket or coat) on its mother's back.

Everyone seemed to enjoy themselves as they belted out the hymns and prayed together. Many of the congregation had marvelous voices; I would have joined in, but the only songs sung in English were for the children.

At the conclusion of the service, Winston and I headed back to the boat to collect George. When Winston and I went ashore, usually he stayed on board *Dove* in case of an emergency. We had been invited for brunch at the home of Cpl. Gerry Smith, the local R.C.M.P. officer in charge of law enforcement at Clyde River. Gerry's partner, Wendel Crosby, joined us for the feast, and what a meal! We were royally treated to a delicious Belgian waffle brunch served up by his pretty wife, Sandy. There were bowls of scrumptious strawberries and blueberries, tangy cheddar cheese, sugary syrup, and—yummy-yum-yum—whipped cream! Washed down with cups of steaming tea and coffee over lively discussions, Sandy's brunch was one of the most delightful I've ever enjoyed. After the amount we devoured, I was surprised when she asked us to return for a taco supper. Gerry allowed us to make phone calls home from his office and to use the shower and laundry facilities. He also gave Winston and George the use of two ATVs to tour the town and countryside. Talk about special treatment! We were definitely spoiled by Gerry and Sandy Smith.

Clyde River (Kangiqlugaapik, "nice little fiord") is set on the low wind-swept shore of Patricia Bay off Clyde Inlet. The population of 650 people depends mainly on government jobs and handicrafts for income. Most Inuit families living in the area are still involved in traditional hunting and fishing activities. According to Gerry, we had just missed a big hunt. A large pod of narwhals had become trapped in the confines of the bay and the whole village turned out for the harvest. "The gunfire was so heavy and going in every direction," he said, "that it was amazing no one got killed."

Later, Wendel took me for a tour of Clyde River and its outskirts, showing me such memorable sights as the airport, the sewage disposal system and, of course, the dump. About a kilometer from the dump, he let Nova, his red Irish setter, out of the police cruiser for his customary run. Tongue lolling, Nova loped along slightly ahead of the vehicle at a steady 20 kph. A large raven swooped down out of nowhere and glided along just above Nova's back until we reached the dump. I was surprised to learn that ravens were year-round residents. I thought that the arctic winter would be far too severe for them to survive.

Wendel told me, "Being a police officer in Clyde River is the same as in any small community. It's hard to fit in. I mainly get to meet the assholes and it's hard to be nice to them when they're usually drunk, belligerent, and breaking the law."

He explained that because of a recent incident involving a former constable, the villagers had become cooler toward the police. The officer was making an arrest when the suspect suddenly wielded a knife. The constable was backed against a wall while many of villagers watched and did nothing. Unable to talk sense into the man, he was forced to draw his gun and shoot in self-defense. I can understand that in a small community, where many people are related, volatile emotions can arise easily.

. I hoped to exchange my shotgun for an Inuit carving, so Wendel introduced me to a white man named John, manager of the Manimiut Store. I couldn't find anything of equal value that I thought Sandra would enjoy, but John taught me some things about the way in which Inuit culture regards children. "The birth of a girl is often looked down upon," John said, "and the child is given away; a boy is thought of as more valuable." He and his young Inuit wife were given such a girl child by her uncle who has six children. "One more girl was just one too many." Another custom is that grandmothers can take full control of raising a baby. John said that this practice is often resisted by the young mothers.

Some time later, I saw John and his Inuit wife walking along the road together. He is much taller than his wife and I smiled to myself as I recalled what he had said about her. "She's an extremely jealous woman with a temper to match. She can go from a mellow 4'10" to a raging 6'8" at the drop of a hat."

When we returned to the police station, Gerry gave us a tour of the jail which consisted of two

George Hone,
Clyde River jail

small cells 2.5 by 3 meters, each containing a cot and a toilet. He told us about a couple of Inuits he had detained for a short time. "Their friends and relatives thought this was a great place," he explained. "They showed up with TVs, VCRs and movies; when they weren't watching movies, they were playing cards."

I expect that in a town as small as Clyde River, Gerry and Wendel both have to be easy going, depending on the nature of the crime. They must try to maintain a friendly standing and avoid being alienated from the community, a tough job under the circumstances.

We spent two days in Clyde River, relaxing, sightseeing and making new friends. Then once again, we hauled anchor and were on our way to our next destination.

Turned Back by Davis Strait

Tuesday, August 29

Departed Clyde River 0100. Winter is fast approaching; the boat is covered with a slight skim of ice. So far, the sea is relatively calm with little or no wind and hopefully will remain this way for some time, enabling us to make a good amount of southward headway. The fog is still thick but there has been little ice.

Wednesday, August 30, 0505 hours

It's been severely foggy all day; besides trying to avoid a collision with an occasional berg, I was frustrated because I could see clear blue skies overhead. The sunlight, although beautiful, created a glare that added to the hazardous fog conditions. During the evening, *Dove* was again covered with a thin layer of ice. When I relieved Winston from his shift at 2200, the fog combined with darkness was extremely hazardous; visibility was down to 15 meters.

Steering by compass is almost totally out of the question and the GPS is slow to react. A star shining through the ratlines on the starboard side appeared like a lamp held by an angel, guiding us safely through the murky fog and treacherous icebergs.

The fog lifted for a short time and exposed numerous icebergs glittering like jewels scattered by a jeweler across a blue satin sea, as if for my inspection. I can see Broughton Island (Quikiq-tarjuaq, "big island") about 18 meters to the south. As we draw near, I shall be vigilant; a good many polar bears are said to congregate in that vicinity.

Thursday, August 31

The day began with sunny skies, calm seas and a mist that contained a few icebergs, but soon sunny became cloudy, calm became rough, and mist became fog. *Dove* managed to slice her way through quite a few kilometers of ice several times throughout the day. Although the sea became dreadfully lumpy and miserable and I was on the verge of seasickness, I was content that we had made fairly good progress although the boat was a little off the desired course.

Winston decided to put into Sunneshine Inlet, just off Cape Dyer, to investigate an abandoned D.E.W. station in hopes of finding some discarded diesel. Having read about near disasters when boats get jammed tight in similar inlets, the idea of putting into a long skinny inlet with a load of pack ice moving right along behind us made me more than a little nervous.

In heavy fog, with night fast descending, I saw three islands near the narrow entrance. I carefully maneuvered *Dove* between two of the islands, straining to avoid hitting one of the many ice floes, when suddenly Castle Island loomed high in front of us, forcing me to change course quickly. We spent a fitful night hooked to a large drifting ice floe.

Friday, September 1

We awoke to a gloomy morning; dark, brooding cliffs stretched into the clouds. The ice, packing in solidly, makes it impossible to reach the D.E.W. line station only 3 km distant. Reluctantly, we leave without any diesel. I suspect from Winston's behavior that he is not a "happy camper" because the previous day's efforts consumed a lot of precious diesel as well as time.

We are motoring back to Davis Strait and a probable repeat of yesterday's gale force winds. Who knows? Perhaps it's blown itself out. We can only hope. At least this morning I comfortably made toast and tea. Yesterday, while preparing pancakes —or splatter-cakes—it was almost impossible to stand in one place, let alone flip them.

Saturday, September 2

There isn't much wind; sea still very lumpy and uncomfortable; not as bad as yesterday when the waves were steep, two and a half meters high. Last night we motored through the fog; it was so dark that it was impossible to see three meters in front of the boat. Pure madness, I thought, to motor blindly when even a small berg could kill us, if we struck it hard enough.

Short on fuel; 865 km to cover before reaching our next destination on the Labrador coast. We attempted to sail today; it was hopeless. The best *Dove* would do was two knots. Only 12 hours of fuel remain; we're hoping for a decent north-westerly to keep us on course and put some kilo-meters under our belts. I mentioned returning to Clyde River to refuel and add additional fuel containers to see us down the Labrador coast; Winston was adamant about not turning back.

I see the fog has lifted; now if only the wind would blow a gentle 10-20 knots out of the northwest. I haven't slept in over 24 hours.

I was seasick yesterday, throwing up three times; as I write, I still don't feel well. I've lost a lot of weight and I worry sometimes about our not-too-nutritious diet.

Sunday, September 3

I think I'm finally over my seasickness; I've been able to keep the little I've eaten down. The wind has been steady but light from the southwest. We made a little southerly headway but lost it by drifting too close to Baffin Island.

While *Dove* self-steered, the ride was not quite so rough and I was able to sleep off and on through the day and night. Since none of us were paying much attention to *Dove's* direction, we came very close to a gigantic iceberg. A sense of hopelessness came over me as we floated around almost aimlessly in Davis Strait.

What we needed was fuel, lots of fuel. With this in mind, I checked out the chart for another destination. Frobisher Bay (Iqaluit) seemed a possibility, but Winston said we should go instead to Pangnirtung in Cumberland Sound. I took one look at the location and realized we did have an option, something to look forward to. Winston didn't like the idea of turning back 240 kilometers and asked George what he thought. I waited anxiously, fingers crossed. George agreed, so we're headed for Pangnirtung.

Monday, September 4, 0435 hours

We are still 144 kilometers from Pangnirtung; the sea is calm and the fog has thinned considerably. Although the day is overcast, all looks well. I do object to Winston's insistence on driving hard when it's dark and foggy and I can't see the bow of the boat. Winston shut the engine down last night, but unless he does so again, I think our situation is precarious and dangerous. I raised the possibility of running into an iceberg and he replied, "It's unlikely we would run into one as we've hardly seen any all day."

To which I replied, "That's what the *Titanic* thought."

PANGNIRTUNG

Arrived 2300 hours, Tuesday, September 5. At the moment we are anchored in front of the small village of Pangnirtung. I look forward to seeing what this place looks like in daylight. Last night, as we motored through Cumberland Sound leaving phosphorescent sparks trailing in our wake, Pangnirtung gradually came into sight. Like stars at nightfall, the lamps of the streets and homes seemed to blink on one at a time to greet us. At first the lights seemed to magnify the town's size, but as we drew closer, it grew smaller. After our ordeal at sea, it will be good to go ashore, purchase some much needed fuel, and simply stretch my legs.

In the morning, Winston went ashore in search of fuel, food and water. When he came back, I was elected to aid in transporting the fuel while George remained aboard *Dove* in case she needed to be moved due to the extreme tides in this area.

While Winston rowed toward the small harbour, I noticed the hustle and bustle along the shore. A huge yellow excavator was noisily dredging the bottom of the harbour, loading its muddy contents into a large dump truck. The fuel tanks were located just beyond the excavation site, so that's where Winston dropped me. Seeing how muddy it was, Winston decided to moor the dinghy along with other boats on the opposite side of the harbour.

Going ashore near the dredging site was not a good idea. However, since I was already there, I tried to walk along the shore to meet Winston. This was a bad move.

As I picked my way across the deeply trenched and rutted surface of the harbour bottom, at first the earth was firm. Before long, conditions changed. I plodded along, one step at a time, until suddenly I sank into the sucking ooze almost to my boot tops. In order to take another step, I was forced to bend down and grab one of my boots to help lift it free from the quagmire. I tried to go back. Going forward was hard enough, but trying to turn while pulling my feet out by hand was impossible.

I went splat on my ass. The grey mud that oozed around my hands and bottom felt surprisingly warm. Cautiously, praying I wouldn't have to crawl or swim out, I pulled myself out of the mud and stood up. I could hear the construction workers laughing at my slapstick performance. When I got back to my starting point, I was greeted by a lot of smiling faces. I did some hard scraping and rinsing to get my gumboots clean; my pants and coat were another story.

The Inuit workers told me I looked like a drunken sailor and there was some truth to what they said. After being at sea for an extended time, especially when it has been unusually rough,

I have a difficult time walking a straight line when on shore. It's not unlike being intoxicated.

Probably because of my odd behavior crossing the harbour, a congenial Inuit man with a wide, bright smile asked me a question.

I didn't understand him, so the Inuit who owned the dredger explained that the man wanted to trade fish for booze. I declined.

While we watched the ooze being excavated, the friendly boss said that when they were dredging the harbour bottom the previous year, the machine had become heavily imbedded in the mud. After many attempts to extract it, in the end he was left with no choice but to watch the tide roll in and swallow it whole. For six days he watched helplessly as the tide continued to roll in and out until some special heavy equipment arrived to pull it free.

"The repairs must have taken a big whack out of your profits," I commented.

He replied smiling, "It cost me $7,000 to fix and I couldn't afford to go on holidays." I think it was the loss of holidays rather than the money which hurt him most, because he went on to say, " I look forward to winter because then I can just kick back; otherwise, it's just like down south, everyone is in a big rush to go nowhere."

We both agreed that the "pencil-pushing people back in Ottawa" had no right to write laws and legislation pertaining to a land, its people and customs when they knew little or nothing about them.

Since a large part of the Northwest Territories will soon be given back to the Inuit, I asked him how he felt about having his own province or country. His eyes brightened and I could sense his pride as he answered: "It's called Nunavut; it means "our

land." At last we can govern ourselves and look out for our land and its animals—they need to be conserved."

He really loved his land. "Sometimes I go to Montreal for a holiday," he told me. "I try to smile and be friendly to people, but they just ignore me. Back here, everyone smiles and says hello."

He's right. I have found that Montreal is not very friendly, especially if English is your main language. On the other hand, I can attest to Pangnirtung's warmth of spirit and friendship. Everyone we met was more than helpful and made us feel welcome.

Pangnirtung, "the place of many bull caribou," is affection-ately called "Pang" by the locals. Approximately 1,000 people, mostly Inuit, live in this stunning setting about 50 km south of the Arctic Circle. High and majestic snow-capped mountains rise steeply from Pangnirtung Fiord; when the sea is calm, a mirror image doubles the beauty.

While Winston, George and I were browsing through the modern Angmarlic Visitor Center observing the nicely displayed Inuit soapstone carvings and old whaling artifacts, we were approached by the manager, Margret Karpik, an attractive Inuit woman. She asked if we would give a talk about our trip at the rec center in the late afternoon. Not being much of a public speaker, I was apprehensive, but since Winston did most of the talking and the crowd was small and casual, I made out just fine.

Right after the talk, we were presented with a small handbook about Baffin Island and treated to delicious caribou stew. Helen Parfit, a school teacher from the audience, invited us to her house for tea and a piece of tasty homemade blueberry-yogurt pie a la mode. During the visit, we each took a turn enjoying the radiant luxury of a bath.

Return to Pangnirtung
Dove Readied for Winter

We left Pang the next day, September 6, at 0205. As the houses clinging to Pang's rocky shore slowly disappeared behind *Dove's* wake, I recalled the words of the friendly truck driver who had filled our fuel containers on the beach. "The winds here are something fierce. You'll notice the houses here have steel cables strapped over them and are bolted to the ground so they won't fly away. See those huge fuel tanks yonder? Well, apparently someone left the door open at the top of one and the force of the wind sucked all the air out, causing a vacuum. The whole thing caved in—almost blew away."

The wind funneling down the fiord between the high mountains has been clocked at over 160 kilometers per hour. I hoped that by the time *Dove* reached Davis Strait, there would be little or no wind.

Thursday, September 7

The sea slowly went from calm to completely berserk. I was back hugging the toilet; impossible to sleep.

Friday, September 8

The wind is blowing 35-40 knots. The seas are dangerous, the odd one breaking over the top of the wheelhouse. Still barfing; no sleep.

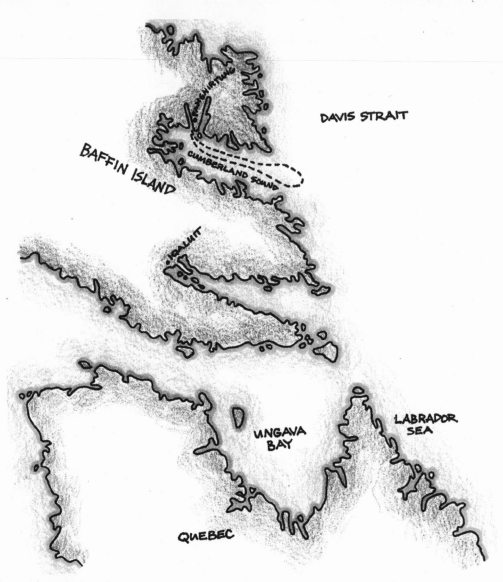

As miserable as I was, I could still marvel at the savagery of a sea gone wild and the frenzy of the wind. I remember one occasion when a large, fast-moving wave hit *Dove* broadside and broke over the entire boat. As I fought with the helm, trying desperately to see through the cascading water, I was amazed at what I saw. Like a woman riding a spirited stallion sidesaddle, *Dove* rode the crest of the huge wave. My adrenaline rushing,

194

I struggled against the wave's power until *Dove* managed to crawl off the crest before being hurled into the boiling chasm. I'd be a liar if I said I wasn't afraid.

Dove hove to during the night with a sea anchor dragging to slow down our drift on the thrashing sea. Seasick, tired and barely caring what might happen, I sat huddled at the foot of George's bunk, my head cushioned on dank heavy-weather clothing, listening to the waves battering against the hull. It was impossible to stretch out or sleep and my thoughts drifted. I wondered if I would ever see home again. The night seemed to last forever.

Saturday, September 9

We are all in agreement; it is too late in the season to make it safely down the Labrador coast. Returned to Pang 1500 hours.

11,500 kilometers, four and a half months later, the trip of a lifetime has ended for Lenny the deckhand.

Although the sailing voyage had ended, we had a lot of preparations to complete before leaving the friendly hamlet of Pangnirtung. The kind and hospitable minister, Roy Bowkett, and his Inuit wife, Annie, gave us the use of a small but comfortable apartment; compared to *Dove*, it was huge and luxurious. This would be our home and headquarters until *Dove* was made secure and weather-tight for the long winter ahead.

Roy and Annie treated us like family; their door was always open. Roy's gourmet suppers, as well as Annie's fresh bannock, were always a delight. On the 17th of September, my 54th birthday, Winston baked a cake, and Annie gave me a gift as well, an intricately sewn pair of miniature mukluks. Annie is an expert seamstress who makes the most beautiful arctic clothing imaginable. I think what I will miss most about Pang are friends such as Roy and Annie Bowkett.

The day before *Dove* was to be hauled out, we left her anchored in the harbour. Unfortunately, she wasn't in quite the proper place for low tide. When we returned a little later, we found her lying on her side. Winston and I rowed out to check for any damage, but except for a couple of boots floating in the water that covered part of the cabin floor, she was in fine shape.

There is no marine ways in Pangnirtung but this didn't faze Winston and Tim Dialla, overseer of the dredging and construction, who helped us. At low tide, a large steel plate was dragged down to the beach behind the breakwater The next day, we floated *Dove* over the plate at high tide; when the tide retreated, she stood high and dry on the center of the plate. We placed braces to hold the vessel upright and Winston made sure that Dove was secure. Then Tim dragged both plate and boat to high ground away from the tide and ice. Except for the loss of bottom paint, a few traces of bare metal, and the odd dent from all her groundings and batterings, *Dove* was in excellent shape. We made sure that all the bracing was reinforced and that the boat would withstand the winter storms.

We spent the next few days moving the remainder of the food stores, electronics, and other incidentals to Roy's attic to await Winston's return the following year. Our personal belongings were crated and shipped home by mail. Lastly, *Dove* was

Readying Dove for the Winter, Pangnirtung

snugly covered with a large tarp and any small openings plugged and sealed to keep out the wind-driven snow. Certain that she was shipshape for the winter, we trudged off. As I looked back one last time, the little boat that had been my home and haven seemed lonely and forlorn; I felt as if I was abandoning a good and faithful friend.

A light drift of snow fell during our last night at Pangnirtung and, in the morning, as we walked across the airstrip from the terminal, it swirled around our feet like white tornadoes. Winter had arrived with our departure.

As the plane sped down the runway and began to lift,

I strained in my seat for one last glimpse of the little hamlet but it had completely disappeared below the clouds. The village, as well as the voyage, seemed to be nothing but a dream, a trick of the imagination.

The plane touched down lightly at Iqaluit (Frobisher Bay), Baffin Island and, after a brief wait and plane change, we were once again airborne, this time aboard a First Air jet headed for Canada's capital city, Ottawa, Ontario. Through occasional openings in the clouds, I surveyed the spectacular serenity of Davis Strait and its armada of diamond-studded icebergs. From that lofty altitude, the sea looked peaceful and it was hard to believe that it had abruptly ended our voyage.

After small arctic villages, Ottawa was a shock. I felt almost alien in my own environment and couldn't wait to leave. Winston and George stayed in Ottawa for several days but I left for home almost immediately.

As my fourth and final flight skimmed across the Strait of Juan de Fuca toward Cassidy Airport, about 20 minutes south of Nanaimo, I felt excitement building. I remembered how it had felt returning from other journeys when there was no one to meet me and I was greeted only by my loneliness, but this time was different. Sandra was there to greet me and we flew into each other's arms and embraced. The journey had ended; I was home.

Epilogue: Reflections from Within

It's been a little over a year since the voyage ended. I live near the center of the city now, in a house. Several galleries are interested in exhibiting my paintings of the voyage. I want to go to sea again, only this time in a kayak, and explore intimately the coastline of British Columbia.

I wasn't much of a sailor when Winston, George and I put out to sea and I wasn't much of one when the voyage ended. The beauty, the grandeur, the harshness—the possibility of perishing—were more than I anticipated.

Sometimes, when I row across the channel to Newcastle Island and walk the windswept rocky beach, I close my eyes and listen to the lap of the sea, and I am back in the arctic regions where trees do not grow.

Once again I walk along a shore where blocks of ice have churned up large chunks of permafrost and every bone has a tale to tell. Terrain that once appeared formidable, bleak and inhospitable invigorated me and I miss it.

I miss the warm greetings and happy smiles of the high-latitude natives. I remember the simple lifestyle of those proud people and yearn for some of that simplicity. We no longer live aboard *Dreamer II* and I miss our small dockside community that evoked the camaraderie of an Inuit village.

I follow *Dove's* route on a chart of the arctic archipelago and I can't believe that I was a part of such an astounding voyage. Yet, as I read the names—Shishmaref, Akoliakatat Pass,

Herschel Island, Gjoa Haven, Tuktoyaktuk, Pond Inlet—in the blink of an eye, I'm there.

I have sailed the vast Arctic Ocean and felt the energy, the very heartbeat of this planet Earth, our home. When the skies merged with the sea and the horizon disappeared, I felt as if I was voyaging into the depths of the universe. At the mercy of Mother Nature, I felt her rage over the degradation of her oceans, lakes and waterways at the hands of humans.

Despite the dangers of wind and waves, polar bears and grizzlies, I felt safer there than strolling city streets. In spite of discomfort, loneliness and seasickness, I would go again if I had the chance.

***

My attempt to put into perspective the wonders and events which took place during the voyage is like taking another journey into the unknown. The weight loss, fatigue and pain I suffered are easily understood, but the causes of my feelings of loss and depression are more difficult to discover. I feel like a child who cries, "It hurts, but I don't know where."

Like a joyful actor who revels in the spotlight, the applause of the audience, I felt intensified and enlivened by the challenges of the voyage. Now the curtain has fallen and my performance has ended. When I realized that I would never experience such a voyage again, I felt downcast and dispirited.

The adventure of living on the edge, exposing one's physical strengths or inner sensibilities, admitting one's vulnerability, creates a natural high and it takes time to wind down, to integrate the experiences and smooth the highs and lows into harmony.

Writing this book has put me in touch with the continuing journey of my own mortality and spirituality. I may not have become a better person, but meeting the Inuit people reawakened my striving toward modesty and humility. They helped me to remember when time itself was more valuable to me than material gain. For the past ten or twelve years, I've tried to live simply and to earn only as much as I need, but old patterns and desires are difficult to break. I now see that my life holds contradictions; there are highs and lows that effect subtle changes in me. The voyage may be over, but my journey continues.

Acknowledgements

I owe a great deal of gratitude to the following people who helped make this book a reality: Winston Bushnell, for allowing me to be a part of his dream to traverse the legendary Northwest Passage; George Hone, a first-rate mate who was always there when things got tough; the Inuit and other people of the high latitudes for their gracious hospitality and friendship; sponsors Tony O'Connor, Director of Hydrography, Pacific Region, Irena Kuna, manager of corporate sales, Far West, Lee Bonar, owner and manager of Harbour Chandler Ltd.; my publishers, Don and Réanne Douglass, my editor, Cindy Kamler, and graphic designers Melanie Haage and Faith Rumm, who steered me through the literary maze; and my many friends and relatives who gave me their support.

Enjoy these other adventure books from FineEdge.com

The Arctic to the Antarctic
Sailing the Edges of the World
By Mladen Sutej

The dramatic account of the first circumnavigation of the North and South American continents.

Cape Horn
One Man's Dream, One Woman's Nightmare
by Réanne Hemingway-Douglass

"This is the sea story to read if you read only one." —McGraw Hill, International Marine Catalog

Trekka Round the World
by John Guzzwell

"John Guzzwell is an inspiration to all blue-water sailors."—*Wooden Boat*

"A classic of small boat voyaging." —*Pacific Yachting*

Final Voyage of the *Princess Sophia*
Did they all have to die?
Betty O'Keefe and Ian Macdonald

This story explores the heroic efforts of those who answered the SOS, at first to save and later to recover the bodies of those lost.

Sea Stories of the Inside Passage
by Iain Lawrence

"I can't wait to read Iain's next sea story; he describes the life of the Inside Passage like no one else."—Sherrill and Rene Kitson, Ivory Island Lightstation

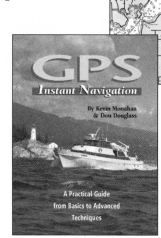

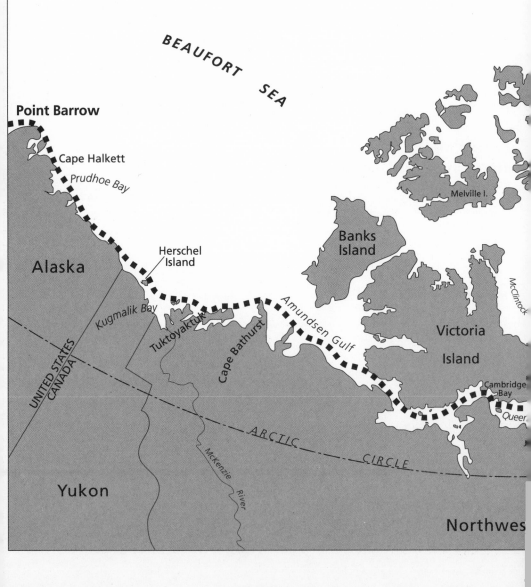